D1468891

1

ALL YOU NEED TO KNOW ABOUT AMERICAN HISTORY

The HuntThePast.com guide through all things
American History

MIDDLE SCHOOL EDITION

By: Zack Edwards

Creator of Historical Conquest: The Card Game
Founder and CEO of Historical Conquest, LLC
Designer, but not writer, of HuntThePast.com
Chairman of the non-profit Community Fix

Dedicated to the many supporters of Historical Conquest, including:

Caylee Edwards
Lynda & Norman Edwards
Jeff Jones
Conor Robison
Bethany Flynn Sosh
Jonathan Dawson
Sione Tupou
Loren Betteridge
Sam & Peggy Edwards
Elan & Aaron Eddington
Sarai and Scott Timothy
The McDonald Family
The Cummins Family
Kay and Trace Waldram
Lisa Imerman
Jonah Hosmer
Vikki Walters
Josh Forsman
Shawnta Ray
Teddi McAbee
Megan Terrell
Raymond Malone
Karen Allen
Josiah Herrington
Brian McMeans
Tammy Foster
Mark Going
Laura Harmon
Jeremy Spouse

Introduction:

This is not just any book about American History. You do not just read this book, you experience it. In this book, you will not just read words, but interact with the book, And you will find more information on each subject by visiting our website, www.HuntThePast.com.

Why connect a website and a book, you may ask? Because there are too many topics and too much information in each unit to fit it into a book. We want you to be caught up in this web of information, diving deeper into topics you may want to know more about. Think of it this way: most curriculum and textbooks give a bird's eye view of an event in history. They never really talk about what is most important, and the most interesting - the people and the moments. Why, you might think, do they not provide as much information as possible? Because it is extremely expensive to produce this content-rich material. Therefore, we are designing this book to entice you to go a little deeper, ask questions, and find out the truth for yourself, not just take the information you are given at face value. We provide you with a bird's eye view from this book, and then tell you what units in our library of historical topics are related to the topic, for you to search out.

For example, in our first chapter we will talk about Mesoamerica, diving deeper into the people who populated this land, including the Olmec, Maya, Inca, and Aztec people. You then get the opportunity to learn more about these groups by searching about these topics on our website. In those online units, you will find fun and thought-provoking text, amazing illustrations and historic images of the topic, fun videos, a map, and activities for each unit that help you remember what you learned. We will also tell you the most appropriate times to use the different games you will find on our Gaming Portal.

This is an experience like no other curriculum out there. We want you to have fun, enjoy what you are reading, be in charge of what you are learning, and thereby remember 70-80% of what you are learning.

So, to begin, start by reading the Chapter. Each unit is limited to just one page, even if there is too much information to share. That way, we don't burden you with too much information. On the following page, for each unit, you will find activities to help you critically think about the information you just read (which will help you remember 70-80% of what you read). When it tells you to look up someone on the HuntThePast website, do that as well. See what you can find out about each of these people and write it down in the space provided for you. Just know, if you do not want to write it down, you can always draw it out. Do not be afraid to write in the margins and doodle. This is your book on American History, and you can look back at it at any time, to remind you of what you learned, and your thoughts.

WHERE IN THE WORLD DID LIFE BEGIN?

Let us begin with the bigger picture. What are the earliest civilizations in the world? Looking at this map, it is said that there are five major cradles of civilization – in other words, these are the earliest, largest civilizations in the world. They include the Erlitou of ancient China, the Indus Valley of India, Egypt - in Africa, Sumerian of ancient Iraq, and the Olmec - in Central America. These are the greatest civilizations established, many thousands of years ago. Please mark them on this map:

What can you find about each of these civilizations?

Erlitou culture of China: _____

Indus Valley of India: _____

Ancient Egypt, in Africa: _____

Sumerian of ancient Iraq: _____

Olmec Civilization, in Central America:_____

7

WHERE DID AMERICA BEGIN?

Where did the story of America begin? Was it with Christopher Columbus discovering the New World, or was it the Norse (known today as Vikings) Leif Erickson? It started well before the Europeans. No one can say for certain when the Americas began. What can be said, is that those who began in America, before European explorers, most likely did not originate from there, either. Instead, they traveled there. Some archeologists believe they traveled over an ice bridge between Russia and Alaska; others believe they traveled across the Atlantic and Pacific Oceans, by ship; and yet others say there are those who lived here when all the continents were one, and stayed when the continents split. We will help you with this question in future chapters. First, label as much of this map as you know.

UNIT #1: MESOAMERICA - Major Civilizations (W1:D1)
(search the bold words at huntthepast.com to know more)

In a land not so far away, near the southern border of Mexico, lived a people of much mystery. The Olmecs are regarded as the first civilization to develop in **Mesoamerica**, one of five cradles of civilization.

The Olmec people were a civilization that began in the lower Mexico area, near 2500 BC, and ended abruptly by 400 BC. Without any known reason for their destruction, they were completely wiped out of existence. Some say it was a great battle that destroyed them; others claim it was a famine or disease in the land. These are two of the great mysteries of most ancient civilizations: where did they come from, and where did they go? Though their exact origin is unknown, some evidence shows that their DNA comes from Africa or the Middle East, and it is believed that they came by sea from an unknown African region.

Though not much is known about their origin, what is known, is that they were a rich and powerful people. They made large, colossal head sculptures of their greatest military leaders, that weighed 5-20 tons and were transported far distances. Now, only 17 exist.

There are small amounts of architecture that stand today - mostly ruins of large cities. There are only a few records found in all the Olmec civilization, written on stone tablets or on their architecture. Their writing looks like ancient hieroglyphs, like those in China and Egypt.

Their culture is based around religion, art, and family. Their leaders may have been both spiritual and military leaders, with a singular god, depicted in a sculpture represented as a feathery serpent, though believed to be in the form of a man. The small amounts of architecture, sculptures, writing, and artwork stand as the only record of what was to be believed to be one of the most powerful ancient civilizations.

Activity #2: Big heads - The Olmecs are best known for their large stone sculptures of heads representing their great rulers. This gave prestige to that leader, knowing that those stones would last for thousands of years.

Your task is to draw one of those big rock heads of your parent. To do this, they must sit in front of you while you draw, or use a picture to draw their big rock head. While drawing, have them tell you a story of their past.

AFTER THE OLMECS – Maya, Inca, and Aztec (W1:D2)
(search the bold words at huntthepast.com to know more)

The origin of other Mesoamerican cultures, including the **Inca**, **Maya**, and **Aztec** civilizations, is also not well known. Though there is an overlap in their existence, there is no record of interaction between the Olmec and the Maya; the Inca were in South America.

Activity #1: Where it all began – These four major civilizations lived all over Central and South America. As you learn about these four groups, come back to this map and mark where the Olmecs, Aztec, Inca, and Aztec lived:

After filling out the map, answer this question: What can you learn from mapping out these groups?

_____

_____

_____

The Maya began to develop their civilization around the same time (700 BC) that the Olmec were destroyed. They lived in southern Mexico and the Guatemala area.

Much like the Olmecs, they were immensely powerful in each of their subcultures. See, the Maya had many divisions and wars between their people. There was no unifying government or culture, but instead, they spread out throughout their land and developed cities around their families. These family units were the most important priority to them, more than their riches and power. Most would live as separate family units in their own villages, dividing themselves from the collective Maya body, to keep these families and their traditions unaffected by the other cities. The center of the Mayan civilization were the large cities spread throughout the country, connected where the people would gather to trade and conduct their religious duties. These cities were connected by dirt paths and roads, made out of hardened materials, like stones.

To the Maya, the government, their religion, and even science were one. They believed their leaders were guided by their god and that their god controlled the science around them. Maya customs were based on three ideas (religion, government, and science).

These larger cities were hubs to the outside world and were controlled by the most powerful families. In these centers, you would find a thriving marketplace of goods from all over. Here, the smaller cities would trade with each other, and those living in the larger cities. People would gather to worship their god(s) at the temples, the center of their Maya faith, and conduct very public ceremonies and events. They were also not against those of other lands coming to visit and trade, even with their different languages and customs. They were very accepting of others visiting and doing business. Even when Europeans came to visit, the Maya allowed them to walk amongst them and trade.

This division between cities, though, caused much strife in their own lands, so much, that they began to war against each other, and rebel against the larger bodies. When the Spanish arrived, though, only a fraction of what had once been a powerful nation was still intact.

How they died off is not known, but two ideas have become popular with historians. One thought is, that because they were only reliant on a small number of local foods, a drought could have slowly destroyed their civilization; or, that the warring nature of the people had them kill off one another, nearing 1400 AD. As for what truly occurred, we may never know, because of the lack of writing of their history. Oral traditions and storytelling became the best-known way to keep records. Like the Olmec, though, some of their writing can still be found in hieroglyphic-like writing, similar to Egypt and other ancient civilizations. Imagine that. You could write your story by doodling. Though back then, they had to carefully chisel out every inch with a sharp object and mallet, or something similar.

Activity: Your Calendar - The Maya are known for their calendar, a large stone tablet telling days of the year. This

calendar would track the seasons with different cycles. The actual calendar had 265 days, but combined with other rotations, it would account for nearly 365. Here are images from the Mayan calendar. If you were to draw a calendar, like the Maya calendar, but with 12 months and 365 days, how would yours look? Draw it here:

The Inca (W1:D3)- Well known for their great structure, even at high altitudes, the Incas became a powerful civilization that rivaled most, yet they had no written language. They did have a way of counting, using knots on cords, but the significance of the cords was lost when those who knew their system were either killed in the Incan Civil War, or finished off by the Spanish. Because their traditions and history were passed down by oral means and storytelling, historians cannot find much about their exact history. Instead, they have found most of their ancient information from their stories and archeology.

One of the greatest accomplishments of the Inca, besides their high and superior structures, was their network of roads that stretched across their kingdom - about 2,250 miles of roads. These would have been used to transport armies and messages, using runners, not used to transport goods to trade. Every man was a farmer, producing his own family's food and clothes, and then trading these resources with locals. Much like the Maya, their cities were places of worship and trade, while the smaller cities were those of families trying to separate themselves from the larger body.

The Inca were known for their religion and their belief in a god for each part of nature: The Sun god, Rain god, and more. They would also prepare and keep their dead leaders' bodies, to give guidance from the afterlife.

Their warlike nature, disease, and then the Spanish, finally ended the rule of their greater civilization.

Activity: Keeping a history by telling it to others was extremely difficult, without the ability to write it down. Ask your parents or guardian for a story of your family. Have them tell you the story at night. In the morning, try to write down what you remember about the story. After you have written the summary, ask that same adult to read your story and tell you, on a scale of 1-10, how close you were to telling the story they told you accurately.

_____

_____

_____

_____

_____

_____

_____

_____

On a scale from 1-10, how close was your writing to the story that was told? _____

The Aztec (W1:D4) - The Aztec were the last great civilization of Mesoamerica. It was started by three nomadic tribes, traveling throughout central Mexico, until they gathered as one body, in 1325. It is said that their god picked this location: a great lake where a legend foretold of an eagle perched on a cactus, which symbolized that this was where they would build a greatest city - Tenochtitlan. The city was built on an island, surrounded by swamp, in Lake Texcoco. They irrigated the swamp and used the dirt to expand their island, adding gardens and surrounding the city with water. This land became the foundation for the greatest city in all of Mesoamerica, with great dirt causeways. As the population grew, many sought their own city-states, where they could worship in their own way, causing a division among the people.

These other cities would still benefit the Aztecs, for they designed sophisticated irrigation and farming methods to produce crops like maize (corn), beans, squash, potatoes, avocados, and tomatoes, and trade them in Tenochtitlan. They would also hunt coyotes, armadillos, turkey, and other wildlife, and use them for trade. There were divisions, but they were still able to work together, most of the time.

This city-state order of the Aztec was formed by two means. First, families left the larger body to build smaller cities, to better control their culture and the raising of

17

their families. The second was more prevalent; they would take over cities that were already established before the Aztecs, and put them under their rule. To keep from endless wars and more lives taken, the cities created treaties and alliances with each other, including the smaller cities against the larger Aztec cities. Their god was very war-like, and the teachings of him pushed them into a constant war-like state.

The story of their god's arrival into the world, and how he ruled, is a tale for the most gruesome movie (see the Aztec unit on www.HuntThePast.com/topics), which gives you a greater understanding of why they are so well-known for their war-like nature, and even conducting of human sacrifices. They believed these two acts (war and sacrifices) satisfied their god's lust for blood. Though they were a war-like people, they also understood the nature of man, and not wanting to kill off their entire city in war, they would send out a group of warriors on either side to fight as if the entire army was with them. They would fight and, if they lost, their city would lose, making the winner's tribe the victor. Those surviving champions, from the losing side, would be sacrificed to their god. These battles were known as the "**Flower Wars**," and they happened throughout the civilization, to promote certain tribal dominance.

While being a civilization that fought each other, they also built great temples, and constructed dams, bridges, and other great structures that stood high into the air. Some of these structures still stand today. Much like the civilizations before them, their large cities were a hub for trade, worship, and cultural ceremonies. Tenochtitlan, lacking land to farm, was sustained through its trade with smaller cities, and taxes - known as tributes - from those they conquered.

Beyond this, their early history is not well known, for their codex of history and all other writings were destroyed when Itzcoatl took power in 1427, starting a new reign with "new people," as he saw it. All former writings were hunted down and destroyed, removing any thought of their past beyond that which could be passed down by oral tradition (storytelling). This is how some were able to preserve the record until the Spanish arrived. When the Spanish came, their friars learned their language and transcribed these stories, preserving them as well as possible, though some items were lost in translation and by being passed down by memory.

During Itzcoatl's reign, he formed alliances between their three largest cities, **Tenochtitlan**, Texcoco, and Tlacopan, with other client city-states, in an effort to take on their greatest rival - the Tepanec - and conquer their capital. When a city or people were conquered, their ruler was replaced by someone who honored the greater alliance, who then forced them to pay tribute to the larger city-state. Because of these burdens, and the vengeance sought by those lesser cities (near 500), who lost the "Flower Wars," a great divide had formed among the people. This anger was so high, that when the Spanish arrived, these rival cities and people (including the **Tlaxcala**, their greatest rivals to the east, and a Republic nonetheless) turned against Tenochtitlan and their newest ruler, **Montezuma**. Within three years, the great civilization of the Aztec fell.

Activity: Aztec god (Feathery Serpent) - Aztec respected and even worshiped the image and statues of snakes. This was due to the representation of Quetzalcoatl, their god. His name literally translates to "feathery serpent." This is also seen as a representation of their god coming from the sky (feathery) and moving among the people (serpent). They even presented **Hernan Cortes** with a sculpture of the serpent, just before he attacked Tenochtitlan; this sculpture is now displayed in the British Museum.

Your task today is to draw your representation of a serpent - one that the Aztecs could respect and honor. Design your image on a separate sheet of paper and then transfer that drawing to cardboard. With cut tissue paper, and other materials around the house, glue feathers onto the drawing to decorate it. Use other materials to make it stand out. Draw it again below:

Journal Entry: Critical Thinking - Now that you know the stories of the civilizations who once filled the lands of Central and South America, what are some of the issues and successes that you see in the telling of each of their stories? What can be learned from what they experienced, and what we experience today? In this journal entry, please answer these four questions:

1. What led to the destruction of the Olmecs, Mayans, Incas, and Aztec people?
2. What were similarities of where their civilizations may have gone wrong?
3. What do you see today that we as a people are experiencing, that mimics their behavior?
4. If we follow this path, seen in question 3, what do you think will happen to the United States?

_____

_____

_____

_____

_____

_____

_____

_____

UNIT #2 - DISCOVERY OF THE "NEW WORLD"
BREAKING THE MYTHS OF THE PAST (W2:D1)
(Search bold words at huntthepast.com to know more)

Well before **Christopher Columbus,** there were people throughout America. Many were nomadic people, who would travel with the changing of the seasons; others were able to build into their surroundings small cities throughout their territory. Many of these tribes worked together to trade or keep to their own areas, while some were war-like, and made their livelihood through attacking others.

Recent archeologists have studied the burial remains of these people and dated them back thousands of years, through a process called Carbon Dating (finding the age through the breakdown of its carbon molecules). DNA tests taken from these remains show many different origins, from Asia to Africa; some, like the **Cherokee**, have DNA markers found solely in Jewish DNA. Because there are very few records of the origin of these people (only oral tradition, by storytelling their history), no one knows how these people, throughout the Americas, came to live here.

Their means of arrival in the Americas is also not known. Some evidence points to an ice bridge that formed between Alaska and Russia, allowing people to follow the mammoth herds to this new land. Others believe in a Pangea, where all the continents were once one, and people moved around the sole continent freely. Evidence, in what records exist, DNA, and oral tradition, tell of them traveling to the Americas using small and great ships. For example, it is thought by many in the Southeast Alaska tribe, the **Tlingit** people, that their stories of creation and culture are remarkably similar to those in Tonga, 9,600 miles away.

So, though we do not know how all the Indigenous people came to the Americas, we can learn of the tribes we already know. Note: the word "Indian" comes from the word "Indios" which may have come because Columbus thought he had found India, or as some linguistics experts have considered, Columbus was Italian and did not speak Spanish well. He may have called the people "Una gente in Dios" or "A people in God", "in God", "in Dios", "indios". The terms "Native American" and "Indigenous" came in the late 1970s. Native Americans have been calling themselves Indians for years, as you will find in the Federal Indian Laws, negotiated with North American tribes. For this reason, we will use all three terms. Also, those far in northern Canada, parts of Greenland, and Alaska, would be called 'Inuit,' or to their people, 'Inuktitut.' These people inhabited the arctic areas of North America.

Leif Erickson - How Europe found America
There were many explorers who arrived before Columbus in the Americas - many we have no record of.

One of the first European visitors to settle in the Americas would have to be **Leif Erickson**, whose family was exiled from Norway, in Northern Europe, because of his grandfather, Thorvald Asvaldsson. Thorvald killed a local tribesman, while seeking vengeance for his kinsmen's death, and was banished from the Scandinavian territories.

Note: You may know these people as Vikings, but they never referred to themselves as Vikings, but rather Norseman, coming from Norway. Any historical record who calls them Vikings should be questioned for accuracy. After being banished, Thorvald sailed west to find a land that had been discovered by another Norseman, by the name of Hrafna-Flóki. He came upon a great island, and when seeing a mountain full of glaciers, declared the land to be called Iceland. His son, Eric Thorvaldsson, or as you may know him, **Eric the Red**, followed in his father's footsteps and was banished for killing another Norseman. He was exiled for three years, as punishment, and in his travels found Greenland. His son, Leif Erickson moved to Scotland for a time, and then, from the tales of another Norse explorer, learned of a land West of Greenland. So, he traveled there to find North America and began the first - but unsuccessful - European settlement in the Americas, and began to do missionary work to the indigenous people.

Long story short, Christopher Columbus was not the first European settler to visit North America, or settle in North

America; Columbus did not even settle North America, since he spent all his time in the Caribbean and northern South America. You can read more about this and Columbus's story in the next few chapters. There were hundreds of tribes throughout North and South America, and we will share the stories of some of the largest and more impactful, in the story of North America, in future chapters. It is easier to remember when you weave them into the story and show how they were part of the founding of what is now America

Activity: Boat Building - Have you ever made a paper boat? Well, you are going to have fun with today's activity! Today we will teach you to fold an origami paper boat, and then test its durability in different weather. Visit HuntThePast.com/SpanishExploration/

Part #2: Look at your origami ship and draw it in the space below. How would it look if it were real?

1. How well did your boat stay afloat? _____

_____

2. What did you learn from folding your ship? _____

_____

Christopher Columbus (Cristobal Colon) (W2:D2)
(search bold words at huntthepast.com to know more)

Have you heard of Christopher Columbus before? Why is he so important? From what you have learned, was he a cruel man, who imprisoned the natives, or a great man who cared about them? Whatever you heard is probably only partially true. Allow me to shine some light on the matter, and let you decide what you think.

Before his voyage – Born in Italy, he grew up working at his father's wool shop. To find independence, he enlisted as a sailor, later joining the Italian Navy and becoming an experienced seaman. The Venetian Navy controlled the Spice Trade in the Mediterranean Sea, while the Portuguese controlled the travel around the southern tip of Africa. Spain controlled neither, but after the war with the Moors (African Muslims, who conquered part of what was to become Spain), in Europe, they found themselves with extra ships and soldiers, and needed to find use for them.

During this time, the idea of the earth being spherical, instead of flat, began to gain popularity. The Catholic church, and their scientists and astronomers, were the first to promote this theory. Some scientists began to promote the theory that the easiest way to India and Asia would be by sailing West into the Atlantic unknown. Though this was only believed by a few, Columbus's friend and priest, Fra Fernan Martins, shared this idea with him. Columbus wanted to test the theory, but needed funding, a ship, and a crew. In 1484, he reached out to Portugal and was rejected, then to Genoa and Venice, and was rejected. He even reached out to the English, and was again rejected. Those that did not

believe this theory were numerous, and continued to spread the word that Columbus and those he worked with were wrong. He was very persistent, and in 1492, **Isabel of Castile and Ferdinand of Aragon**, joint rulers of what was to become Spain, decided to support his venture with their excess ships and soldiers.

First Voyage - Columbus guided the Nina, the Pinta, and the Santa Maria, and hired a full crew and all the provisions they believed necessary, then sailed West. Their calculated distance would be short 8,000 nautical miles and with two continents in their way, but what they found would change the world. His crew included the **Niño Brothers** - well trained sailors - whose father came from Africa. His sons were raised master sailors, and with the help of friends, joined Columbus's voyage.

As Columbus continued to sail through these uncharted waters, the men became restless and almost mutinous, but on October 12, 1492, they spotted land. When they reached the sandy shores, they honestly believed they had reached Asia. They planted a cross and dubbed the area San Salvador. They met with the **Taino,** whom Columbus called "Indios." Because of their hospitality and openness, he wrote in his journal that "a better race there cannot be." Columbus's first observation was that they seemed not to have the tools to protect themselves and had to fight in other ways. Due to their intellect and strong builds, Columbus believed the Taino people would be excellent help, and so enlisted - and paid - a few of them to join their efforts. That winter, with the help of some of the Taino, they built their fort. They also worked to convert them to Christianity. He saw them as equals, and advocated for them having equal rights with the Spaniards.

Sailing around the islands of Cuba and Hispaniola, the Santa Maria ran aground. Columbus decided it was time to return to Spain, and restock supplies. He left a few dozen men in their settlement, with guidance to continue building their settlement, and sailed back to Spain. He brought with him goods from the new world, which began the **Columbian Exchange,** and natives as dignitaries, or Ambassadors, to present to the queen. When they arrived, he received a hero's welcome and was rewarded with more money, supplies, and help for his next journey. He was called Admiral, and was made Governor over the new land he had found.

Throughout his many voyages, his most notable creation was the first global trading system, called the Columbian Exchange, where they traded plants, spices, and crops from around the new world, with the European and African markets. This was the driving factor that changed the future of America forever.

But, when he returned to the new world, what he found would boil, and chill, a normal man or woman's blood, all at the same time. The horrors that he would find would cause a chain reaction in the new world...

Activity #1: Columbian Penny Trading Game – First, you need a penny. Go to a relative or a friend and ask them what they would give you for a penny. Then take that item and ask a neighbor or other friend what they would trade you for that new item? You can also trade one item for two, or two for one. You can then trade those items separately as well. What can you acquire after nine trades? Mark down what you would have paid for that item. Remember that you do not need to accept the trade they offer; ask for the biggest and best.

1. Starting with a penny...

2. Traded it for _____. Your value: $_____

3. Traded it for _____. Your value: $_____

4. Traded it for _____. Your value: $_____

5. Traded it for _____. Your value: $_____

6. Traded it for _____. Your value: $_____

7. Traded it for _____. Your value: $_____

8. Traded it for _____. Your value: $_____

Columbus's Second Voyage (W2:D3) - Returning to Hispaniola, he found that the men he left were slaughtered by another tribe, Caribs - who were recorded to be cannibals - and that they had abducted Taino women, and enslaved and harvested others. Dr. Diego Alvarez Canca, a physician who accompanied Columbus on this voyage, journaled their visit to a Carib village, likely on the island now known as St. Thomas. He wrote of the horrible things they did to the women and how they cannibalized the bodies of the fallen.

It was here that Columbus raised up arms against those tribes of other islands who would attack the Taino and his men. At this time, most of the tribes were going through a cultural revolution and beginning to speak the same language - Arawakan; even the Caribs of the local islands began learning the language of their captives. The Caribs themselves were a conquering people, who travelled north from mainland South America and began conquering the many Caribbean islands they came upon on their journey north. Note: up to 20% of the indigenous population were already enslaved by other tribes before Europeans arrived. From there, the relationship between the indigenous and the Spanish soured, from peace and help, to war and resistance. Columbus ordered that those who fought against the Spanish and were captured would not be killed, but imprisoned and shipped back to Spain, to be "civilized." Nearly 550 indigenous people, some captive, and some volunteers, traveled back to Spain when he returned from his second voyage. Beyond the Spanish taking up arms against the Caribs, the natives began to die by the dozens, due to diseases brought from Europe that the Spanish were accustomed to, but the natives were not.

Before leaving, Columbus completed three significant acts in the new world. First, he fortified the entire island of Hispaniola, building a second fort with soldiers and Taino working together. With their guns, horses, and other arms, they had subdued the tribes of the surrounding area. So, the second was to send Friar Ramón Pané to live among the tribes, learning their language and writing down their oral traditions, as the first anthropologist. The third was to begin the search for gold, ordering the Taino to do manual labor. Columbus returned to Spain and presented his findings.

Third Voyage - When he returned on his third voyage, things had turned for the worst. Columbus was commanded to bring back representatives of the crown who despised him. Quickly, Columbuss enemies turned his loyal men against him. One such enemy, Francisco de Bobadilla, was a judge that was to observe Columbus in the new world. He sailed on Columbus's third voyage as an Embassy of the Crown, and friend to the Queen. In 1500, soon after arriving, he charged Columbus with brutal treatment of the native people and tyrannical control over his men. Whether this is true, no one knows, because there are two opposing stories; Columbus's journals and detailed documents from supporters and observers give one side of the story, including that of Friar Ramón Pané, who spent two years writing the stories of most the natives, and a 42-page document written by Bobadilla, with statements of witnesses.

Columbus was quickly imprisoned and shipped back to Spain. The crown took control of the colony, which had been under the governance of Columbus and his brothers. A few months later, all charges were dropped and Columbus was released, due to opposing evidence. He was then provided a fourth voyage.

Fourth Voyage – This is where most historians and textbooks stop, but the most interesting things occur in his fourth voyage. When Columbus returned to Hispaniola, they found that the Spanish had started slave raids and were enslaving the natives by the thousands. War had broken out among all the islands, and the indigenous people were dying by the hundreds. His replacement, Governor Francisco de Bobadilla, who accused Columbus of mistreating the indigenous people, was imprisoned by **Juan Ponce de Leon,** to be shipped back to Spain for misrepresenting Columbus, and for his mistreatment of the native people. The queen was not fond of slavery, or the mistreatment of natives. Columbus requested port in Hispaniola, because of a hurricane he was predicting, but was denied any help by the new Governor. At the same time, a fleet of 30 treasure ships left Hispaniola heading for Spain, not believing Columbus's prediction. 29 were lost at sea, with over 500 men - one being Bobadilla, without telling his side of the story to the Crown.

Columbus spent some time sailing among the islands of the Caribbean, possibly reaching even the coast of Honduras and Panama, and was stranded for a year in Jamaica. Winning favor of the natives, they paddled canoes to Hispaniola, asking the Spanish to rescue Columbus, but the new Governor, Nicolás de Ovando y Cáceresthen, who despised Columbus, denied any help. Later, another ship found Columbus and his men. He returned to Spain, to live the rest of his life.

Activity #2: Thought Experiment: This experiment is to make you think and to be more reflective. Have you been accused of something that was not true? Tell us:

_____

_____

Have you ever been accused of something that was true? What was that instance? Tell the story:

_____

_____

How were the feelings you felt different each time? How did you react differently?

_____

_____

When you look back, and you heard someone's side of their story, and you told your side, were they the same? How did they usually differ? Who was usually believed?

_____

_____

_____

Things are not always what they seem, or there may be more to the story than you hear from one side. It is said that the "victor writes the history." Then the question becomes, who was right? Was Columbus a tyrannical dictator over his men and the Taino, like his enemies wrote, or did he respect the tribe? Think on this?

Treaty of Tordesillas (W2:D4) – On Columbus's return from his first voyage, he stopped by Lisbon, Portugal, to report to King John II that there were more islands west of the Canary Islands. Portugal had no idea Columbus was traveling west and this set off the King, because the treaty they were currently under, he felt, was not being followed with Columbus's new journey. The Treaty of Alcáçovas, signed in 1479 between Portugal and Castille (Spain), had ended their war and allowed Portugal to conduct all sea-based exploration over the Atlantic. King John II sent an angry letter to King Ferdinand and Queen Isabella to denounce what they had done, and to warn them that he was sending an Armada to take the land.

The Spanish fleet was much smaller than Portugal's, so they sought a diplomatic resolution and asked Pope Alexander for a solution, as both countries were Roman Catholic ruled. On May 4, 1493, the Pope decreed, in the Treaty of Tordesillas, that all newly discovered land west of the Canary Islands, if they were made Christian lands, would be safe from any attacks by Portugal, and would give Spain the ability to explore. This created a latitudinal line down the middle of the Atlantic Ocean, dividing the non-European world between Spain and Portugal. John II was not happy, as he believed it gave Spain more land to

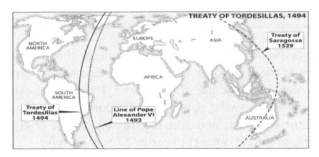

explore, but since everyone believed Columbus had found a few islands, it was not enough to go to war.

In 1500, during the Portuguese search for another route to India, Pedro Álvares Cabral sailed straight into Brazil and sent word to Manuel I, King of Portugal, that there was land inside the line. The king swiftly sent ships to conquer the land. This would later become the country of Brazil, which now speaks Portuguese as their official language, instead of Spanish.

Note: This separation did not apply when the two kingdoms of Portugal and Spain were joined under one crown, in 1580, until 1640. Afterwards, the lands were redivided under this previous treaty. The French, English, Dutch, and Swedes did not recognize this ownership of North and South America and continued to take unclaimed - and even Spanish claimed - lands.

Activity: Exploration Lines - How would you have divided exploration of the globe? In this activity, you are to divide the world into two areas, one part for a classmate or family member, and one for you. What would be fair? Next, ask them if that was a fair divide? Negotiate with them to come to an agreement that is acceptable to both, and draw it on the map below.

Divide the World Equally Between Two Kingdoms

Journal Entry: Was Exploration Morally Wrong? — There is much controversy over the Spanish exploring the Americas and settling the areas they found, not to mention the other countries that will be soon mentioned. Was it right for Europeans to explore the Americas, conquer the indigenous people, and take over the American continent? If not them, then what would have happened to the Americas, if not touched by Europe? Take some time to think about it and write your thoughts in your journal. Tell us what you think:

Write your Journal Here:

_____

_____

_____

_____

_____

_____

UNIT #3: IGNORANCE - "Spanish Protectors" (W3:D1)
(search bold words at huntthepast.com to know more)

Finding a New Land - Imagine you were an explorer and came upon a land that, to the best of your knowledge, was a specific land you expected to be your destination. The ocean is so vast, and the islands are so spread apart, that - as far as you could see - there was no larger body of land. So you stay close to the land you know. Your ignorance does not stop there. You stumble upon a native tribe, never influenced or visited by someone like you before. It could have easily been, to the Spanish, that there were no American continents. Columbus had only found these islands, full of resources, to show the people who paid for his voyage.

There was so much ignorance on the part of the Spanish, as they ventured into these new lands. Both the indigenous people and these explorers knew nothing of each other, and may have worried - on both sides - if they would be captured and taken as slaves. Because their languages were so vastly different, they struggled to understand each other. They worked together to build their first fortification. The Spanish paid the Taino who helped them with manufactured goods, like glass beads.

The worry of the Taino perhaps came to reality when Columbus left a small number of men to continue to build, and left to return to Spain. These men, who possibly had ill intentions, may have turned on the people, and begun to demand - and then plunder - the tribe's goods; and then possibly began abusing their people. There was nothing the Taino could do but defend themselves. Or, maybe... the men who were left did not take anything, but another war-like tribe, like the Carib, came to attack them. The details are not clear, for the men were slaughtered when Columbus returned, and all he found was a broken fortification and bodies.

Now, since they spoke different languages, what was Columbus to think about what had happened? That his men were attacked, which then began a war with the Taino. Again, the Taino may not have had anything to do with it, but according to Columbus and the Spanish ignorance, there was only one group of indigenous people in the area. So, the Spanish could have begun to take up arms against anyone on the islands, and when war struck up against the islanders and the Spanish, they both were forced to defend themselves.

Of course, the claim of brutality would have come from the stronger of the two groups, so the Spanish were to be blamed for what would occur. So who really was at fault? Do we know, since no one today lived back then.

Remember, the native women were rescued from the Carib, by Columbus's men. Could it be that there were no ill feelings between the Taino and Columbus, but they communicated that another tribe had come and killed both of their people and stole their women? Most likely, this is what occurred because Columbus's physician reported back their rescue efforts against the Carib tribe, on what was to become St. Thomas Island, and what the women had communicated to them. It was at this time that Friar Ramón Pané began living among the tribe.

There was one other issue that the Spanish were completely unaware of, that made things hard to understand in the new world. They may have believed that all those that they came upon were of the same tribe. Some tribes spread out among many islands. The Taino people spoke Arawak, but so did the Carib, for there was a cultural shift happening at that time among those that lived among the Hispaniola and surrounding islands. The shift was caused by the Caribs traveling to the Taino's islands, attacking them, stealing their women, and marrying some. The Taino women spoke Arawak, so the Carib needed to learn to communicate with their wives, and so were taught Arawak. To the Spanish, those who spoke the same language were the same people, right?! That was how it was in Europe. So, there was no way for them to tell who was who, until years later, when the Catholic friars came to and began to learn all their languages and cultures.

These friars would live among the people of many different tribes, learn their languages, and work to preserve their history, writing down their oral stories. Combined with this writing, even sometimes ignorant of Columbus and the Spanish, we base what we know from the writings we have. You may not agree with everything or anything they said, but you cannot discount their words. They lived it; historians try to reconstruct it, and we hopefully seek to learn from it.

This is why primary sources, including journals, letters, logs, and other writings from the time, are important sources. A historian from today can only assume they understand what was going on hundreds of years ago, only through writings and small archeological finds. They can only work with their assumptions.

Activity: Coming Upon a New Land – You have been sailing for two months straight, and you feel that you will never find land. Suddenly, a sailor from the crow's nest – a platform at the top of the mast – yells "LAND HO!!!". What would you have experienced in that moment? What would you have experienced when you stepped out of the row boat onto the gritty sand? What would you have experienced when you met the inhabitants of the island? Tell us how you imagine your experience would be, or the journal entry you would have written.

_____

_____

_____

_____

_____

_____

_____

_____

_____

_____

_____

The Ignorance of the Tribes: Visitors Arrive (W3:D2)
(search bold words at huntthepast.com to know more)

You are going about your normal tasks, hunting or harvesting food for your family, when you look upon the horizon over the vast sea and spot clouds low upon the water, coming your way. These are not like any other clouds, but very solid and bright white clouds as the sun beats off them. As they come closer, you see a large canoe traveling underneath them and it is slowly coming closer. As they come close to the island, the clouds begin to shrink, and you see large trees on top of the canoe where the clouds have been put away. It takes hours, but soon the visitors from the canoes board smaller canoes, and begin to paddle into shore.

You are fascinated at this view, and as the visitors come closer, you see two distinct things about them. First, their dress is very strange to you - almost every part of their bodies is covered; and second, the visitors are all men. They beach their canoes and step out of them with clothing on their feet.

Your chief greets them, trying to communicate with them, though it is difficult. They use hand gestures and your chief understands a little from their movements. You feel fear of these new people, and at the same time, fascination to learn more of them; so, when they want to talk to you, you struggle to communicate with them. As a gesture of friendship, you share some of your crops and crafts. You know they are different, and until now, you see no danger from them, though you are cautious. You have seen tribes from other islands come and attack, kill, and enslave the people of your tribes and wonder, will these visitors do the same?

They come in and ask for land, where they can set up a few huts, and this seems acceptable to your chief. How long they will stay is unknown to you, but to keep good will, when they ask for help building their huts, you decide to volunteer. They offer trades as payment: clear beads that sparkle in the light, along with other supplies that did not come from nature.

This seems to be a good relationship, so when the next visitors, much like the first, come to visit, you desire to help and trade with them. Yet, they are not as friendly as the first, and they - like the other tribes - begin to enslave your people.

Activity: How would you feel? – Now tell us your experience from the Taino's eyes? If they were to tell their story, what do you think they would have said?

_____

_____

_____

_____

_____

_____

_____

You are Now a Young Archaeologist - Imagine you are an Archeologist. You have just come to the island of what was Hispaniola. You have read the records of the explorers, different friars who were there at the time, and those that came afterwards. Some wrote their story, others learned the native language and wrote their stories. What are you to expect, looking into these accounts? Where would you begin to look for more information, for further studies? You could find ruins of old forts or villages; ancient weapons that may have lasted, such as spear heads - if they even used heads on their wooden staffs; you could talk with those who still live today, but you know there would be an increased bias to one side. The Taino and Caribs were all extinct by that point. There is always going to be an ignorance of the past when there are competing records, and no written language from the Taino, who experienced it.

The best you can do is try to put all the pieces together, but as you go through the adventures of the Spanish through this new world, you will need to keep an open mind, that it is extremely hard to know what truly happened. It is said that in war, history is written by the victor, but there are always two sides of the story. Our task, as young archeologists (that's you), is to keep an open mind, and while learning these things, try to open your perspective to what happened, according to records, and what could have happened. If no one knows for certain, then an open mind is much more valuable than someone who says, "this is what happened and that is the only way." Do not trust that a human can recall anything exactly how it occurred.

Activity: Aliens Anthropologists - Since there are few places left to be explored on the earth, we will have to use our imagination for this experiment. Imagine you are an alien, coming to earth for the first time. You stumble upon your house, to find a perfectly preserved sample of what life was like here on earth when humans inhabited the planet (humans are now extinct). You are to act as an archeologist, to discover what life was like on this planet.

Example: You enter this inhabitation, and walk into a large gathering area. You see moderately sized structures in the middle of the room. Due to the indentations in the materials, it could only be places the inhabitants would have sat. These structures are encircling a box at the far end of the room, as if that was an object of worship. They must sit there every day and worship the box, for every house in the vicinity has one. All around the box, there are remnants of food scattered among these structures, even on top and within the crevices around where they would have sat. It must be accurate, from the wear on the cushions and the variety of food that has collected, that this was a common area of gathering and worship, maybe even sacrificing the food to the box at the focus of the room.

Now, what items would you have found around your house? And what would you have assumed, as an archeologist, if you would have found them hundreds of years in the future?

Item #1 (describe the item) _____

and it must have been used for (make up a possible use)

_____

_____

_____

_____

Item #2 _____ and it must have

been used for _____

_____

_____

_____

Item #3 _____ and it must have

been used for _____

_____

_____

_____

Item #4 _____ and it must have

been used for _____

_____

_____

_____

What would this have told you about the people who

lived in your house? _____

_____

_____

_____

_____

_____

_____

_____

_____

_____

The Spanish Protectors of America (W3:D3) - Queen

Isabel recognized all those among the islands as subjects - people under her rule - of her country Castille. She believed that they must be treated with care, and not cruelty, and not enslaved, unless criminal conduct had occurred. She believed also that they should be taught Christian ways, but they should not be forced upon them. She sent protectors - friars, to teach the people, and to report back any instances of mistreatment towards the indigenous. After Columbus's first voyage, the Pope also recognized Columbus as the Governor and entrusted him with friars.

In 1515, well after Columbus's death, one Spanish noble, **Bartolome de las Casas,** gave up slavery and became a Dominican friar. He began to write down his view of the treatment of the native people and cruelties that may or may not have occurred. He was accused of overly dramatizing events to push his anti-slavery agenda. He provided more sources of information about the early Americas - a **historiography** (written understanding), though his writings of Columbus were not by observation, but from others' accounts, making this close, but not a primary source. He disdained the treatment of the native people and wrote adamantly against it, requesting to switch African slaves for natives.

Francisco de Vitoria, on the other hand, never visited the Americas and relied upon the writings of other friars to obtain his stance on the people of the Americas. His importance is found in his lectures at the University of Salamanca, and in statements made to the Crown. With Las Casas's help, they created "**The Nueva Laws of 1542,**" regulating the treatment of the indigenous.

Activity: You Make the Laws – What are some of the rules you would have made during this time of exploration? Remember that your people, the Spanish, English, or French, needed to expand (in their eyes). How would you satisfy their need to explore, and yet be just to the indigenous people?

1._____

2._____

3._____

Put yourself in the place of the explorers or settlers; would your rules seem fair to you?

_____

_____

_____

_____

Put yourself in the place of the indigenous people; would your rules seem fair to you?

_____

_____

_____

Amerigo Vespucci and the Naming of America (W3:D4)
(search bold words at huntthepast.com to know more)

Did you know that America was named after a procurer of wine, women, and tax collecting? Amerigo was born in Florence and grew up in mere poverty, yet found employment with the wealthy banker, Lorenzo di Pierfrancesco de **Medici**. Medici used Vespucci to get things that he wanted, whether it was payments by someone, or goods for entertainment. With this experience, Vespucci became a small-time, but successful, businessman, though he knew that his love was the sea. He changed his focus towards ships, as a pilot, navigator, explorer, and cartographer – or map maker. He made his way to Spain and made friends with the man who was in charge of the finances and supplying for Columbus's voyages.

Here, his love for the sea grew. But, being inexperienced, he had to learn quickly, by writing down his observations. He would sell his writings each time he returned to land. One of his responsibilities was cartographer, or map maker. He would use his ability of observation and star-based navigation to create very accurate maps of the New World.

His writings became so widespread throughout Europe, that he was just as well-known as Columbus himself. He made the claim of this being a "New World" and it began to stick - the idea that this was not Asia, but a new continent, instead. Working for both the King and Queen of Spain, and their rival Portugal, he was able to take two long voyages and travel most of the eastern coast of South and Central America. His maps were to become so well-known, that a German cosmographer created the first world map, 'Cosmographia Waldseemuller,' published the year after Columbus's death, naming the new continent America (after Amerigo Vesupucci, who died before the name stuck).

Activity: Recognition - If you could name something after yourself, what would it be? Remember that, to name something after yourself, you have to have influence over it, and others must recognize that. With that recognition, what would you give your name to?

1. _____

2. _____

3. _____

Part 2 – If you were to name the new world of the American Continent, what would you name it? Allow at least two of those names to be named after you. What would the name be?

1. _____

2. _____

3. _____

4. _____

Journal Entry: Who is at Fault if anyone? – The world was changing quickly at this point in history, and someone is the first to do almost everything that occurred during this time. Who's fault is it? This can be on any topic mentioned in the last week. Whose fault was it for strife in indigenous society, Spanish or other native tribes? How about death and disease; if it wasn't the Spanish, would it have been another country? Take some time to think about it and then write down your thoughts in your journal. Tell us what you think:

Write your Journal Here:

_____

_____

_____

_____

_____

_____

_____

UNIT #4 – WORLD EVENTS AT THIS TIME... (W4:D1)
(search bold words at huntthepast.com to know more)
EUROPE:

The Medici Family takes over Florence (1512) – The Medici household was a powerful group of people, whose influence was in finance, banking, and politics. They grew in power in the Republic of Florence, which would later merge into the country of Italy. Their influence extended throughout most of Europe, including working with Columbus to finance his journey, through the help of Amerigo Vespucci. The Medici Bank was the largest bank and financier in all of Europe. From this family came four popes (Pope Leo X, Pope Clement

VII, Pope Pius IV, and Pope Leo XI), two queens of France (Catherine de' Medici and Marie de' Medici), and many other members of royalty. Through the spread of their power and influence, they filled the seats of Florence's government, until they eventually took over the city. Florence became a thriving environment for art and humanism, inspiring the Italian Renaissance. Their patrons included Botticelli, **Leonardo da Vinci**, **Michelangelo**, **Raphael**, **Machiavelli**, and **Galileo**. It was here that **Machiavelli**, a philosopher and historian, became "the father of modern political philosophy and political science". His book, *The Prince*, helped guide his political philosophy, and showed him how it was full of deception, treachery, and crime. He remained influential after the Medici fell.

The Italian Renaissance – There are many Renaissances that occurred, around the 15th to 17th centuries, throughout the world. This was a transition period, out of the Middle Ages, to more of the modern era. The European Renaissances were a time of cultural, artistic, political, philosophical, and economic "rebirth". Some of the greatest minds became famous and thrived during this time, including authors, statesmen, scientists, and

artists. Some of these included **Michelangelo, Leonardo da Vinci, Raphael, William Shakespeare, Sandro Botticelli, Nicolaus Copernicus, Martin Luther, John Calvin, Johannes Gutenberg, Niccolò Machiavelli, Lorenzo de Medici, Paracelsus, Thomas More,** and **Johannes Kepler**.

During this period, global exploration opened Europe to new lands, cultures, and commerce. It was considered the "**Age of Exploration.**" It was during this time, that every part of the map was to be explored, including the Americas, Africa, Asia, Antarctica. In each of these lands, sailors found new goods to sell, and to present to the royalty who allowed their ventures. The two greatest countries for exploration started with Portugal and Spain, and soon expanded to the British, French, Swedes, and Dutch.

Gutenberg and his Press (1440) – One of the greatest inventions during the Renaissance was the **Gutenberg Press**. Although there were many presses for printing made around the world, including those in China and other manual presses, Gutenberg's was made for mass

 production of literature - more than ever before. The one book that was published by this press, and really made Gutenberg famous, was the first printing of the **Gutenberg Bible**. Before that point, only the clerics and the wealthy held a copy, and most of those were handwritten and illustrated. Only after the press was created were the average (though still, sometimes wealthier) person able to own a copy of the Bible. This allowed the layman to study their scriptures, which turned many against the Roman Catholic Church, because it was now open to more interpretations.

The Reformation (1501-1550) - Some of those famous for interpreting the Bible and fighting against the church, included **Martin Luther**, who wrote the 95 thesis, and **John Calvin**, who promoted the **Reformation** throughout France and the separation of Christianity from Catholic beliefs. Opposition to some of these "radical" views included **Thomas More,** a staunch supporter of Catholicism, who attacked **King Henry VIII,** for wanting a separation of the  Catholic church and state. The King declared himself the supreme head of this new church - the Church of England. Henry VIII soon convicted, and later executed,

More for treason, for not accepting the Oath of Supremacy and allowing Henry to divorce Catherine of Aragon, among his other **Wives**.

Heliocentric Solar System (1514) – Another great

breakthrough, beyond religion and exploration, came from science. One of the greatest discoveries during this time was the **Heliocentric Solar System**, or the understanding that the earth and all planets revolved around the sun, as opposed to geocentrism, which placed the earth at the center. This also opened many minds to the knowledge that the earth was spherical, and so there was no edge of the earth of which to fall off.

Astronomers such as **Nicolas Copernicus,** who led the Copernican Revolution - stating the earth and all planets revolved around the sun, became one of the first and most popular astronomers to deny the thinking of the past. **Johannes Kepler**, the German Mathematician, took from Copernicus's design and developed the Law of Planetary Motion and helped break apart the ideas of Astronomy and Astrology. He also published a strong argument for how God controlled the heavens with

Math. **Galileo Galilei**, was the father of observational

 astronomy, modern physics, and the Scientific Method. Though many myths have arisen about his stance against the Catholic church in promoting modern science, these are not true, for only a few years after he published his theory, in 1611, a team of Jesuit astronomers - called Society of Jesus, started by **Ignatius of Loyola** - confirmed his findings. He instead, did not deny religion for science, but instead exclaimed the divine control over science, and how they worked together. Pope Urban VIII and the Jesuits supported his theories.

There was still a battle that was brewing between scientists, those who supported Galileo, and those who supported Tycho Brahe's theory of planetary motion. Galileo also claimed that the tides of the Atlantic only happened once a day, due to gravitational pulls as the earth moved around its axis, which was false; it was twice. It was this battle between scientists that caused a rift between Galileo and the church, though he never lost his faith, but instead in other scientists who testified against him in the Roman **Inquisition. Francis Bacon** developed modern scientific method. The Renaissance became the period of scientific and philosophical thought.

The Spanish Inquisition and Renaissance Justice (1478) –

The Spanish Inquisition was a judicial system, or court, sanctioned by the Pope, but established by **Queen Isabel** of Castile and **King Ferdinand II** of Aragon, to be separate from the Medieval Inquisitions, which was under Papal rule. It was the most substantial inquisition of the three - including the Roman Inquisition and Portuguese Inquisition. It was to be conducted only in Spain and Spanish colonies, among the Americas. One of its goals was to identify and repel heresy among those who converted to Catholicism, from Judaism and Islam. This was intensified when a decree came from the queen that all Muslims and Jews must convert to Catholicism or leave Castile peacefully. The inquisition was also known to have taken up the task of removing witchcraft, but would not go as far as to use

the **Malleus Maleficarum**, a book that was designed to spot witchcraft. The Inquisition condemned this book as unethical, and the use of illegal procedures and Catholic doctrine of demonology. The Inquisition, however, did accept torture to extract confessions. In 1834, Queen Isabella II abolished the Inquisition.

Northern European Renaissance –

During this time, there were many different Renaissances, caused by a domino effect of other countries influencing each other, including that of Germany, France, England, Low Countries (Netherlands), and Poland. Much of this was due to commerce with those experiencing the Italian Renaissance. The feudalist system, which had dominated Europe for a thousand years, had declined, partially due to **the Plague** which spread throughout Europe after the Crusades. This Renaissance also came, in part, from the weakening of the Roman Catholic Church over much of Europe, and was intricately linked to the Protestant Reformation. This was also the time of **King Henry VIII** and his successor, **Bloody Queen Mary**, who established power through brute force and bloodshed.

Activity: A House Torn in Two - Every house has disagreements. Ask your parents if they will allow you to make the decision in one of their future discussions, whether it is where your family will go on a Saturday, or where you will go out to eat. Ask them if you can be the judge, and allow your parents or siblings to try to convince you of their side. Pretend you are in court and must make the final decision on a fair, unbiased basis, which also means, it doesn't matter what you want, but whoever makes the most logical argument wins.

What decision did you discuss with your family?

_____

What was Side #1, and what was their argument?

_____

_____

What was Side #2, and what was their argument?

_____

_____

How did you make your decision?

_____

_____

ASIA (W4:D2):

Ottoman Empire (Middle East: 1299 - 1922) – While the Renaissance was occurring throughout Western Europe, most of the surrounding areas around the Mediterranean, some of the Middle East, and even

Northern Africa, was controlled by the Islamic **Ottoman Empire**. Constantinople was conquered in 1453, Cairo in 1526, and Algeriers in 1528. **Suleiman the Magnificent** was the longest lasting monarch, during most of the European Renaissance. The Ottomans continued to attack Christian-controlled Europe, taking more areas from Europe. Suleiman took many Christian strongholds, including Belgrade and Rhodes, and conquered much of Eastern Europe, until the Siege of Vienna. He controlled most of the Mediterranean, Red Sea, and the Persian Gulf, which controlled much of the spice trade for Europe. He also annexed much of Iran and Northern Africa. He sold millions of slaves; many white Christian Europeans captured in battle were sold in the African slave markets, as well. The Empire would also capture women and children, and sell them into slavery. He broke from Ottoman tradition, though, when he married an Orthodox Christian woman slave, from his harem. She converted to Islam, and yet always stood out, due to her firey red hair. She is known by the West as Roxelana. Only one of his sons, born to Roxelana, succeeded him, since the Sultan executed two of his sons, and the others died of Smallpox. After his death, the Ottoman Empire went through economic and political changes, called the Transformation.

The Persian Safavid Empire (Iran: 1051-1736) – This was one of Iranian's greatest Empires, after Muslim conquered Persia (7th Century). It was ruled by the Safavid dynasty and was in constant battles with the Ottoman Empire, as they both continued to fight to expand their reach. The Ottoman were of Sunni Muslim rule, as opposed to the Safavid, who considered their empire a Shi'ite state.

The Chinese Renaissance (China: 1368 – 1600) – During

this time, Europe's influence grew throughout Asia, including that of European merchants and Christian missionaries visiting China. **The Ming Dynasty** had reached its peak, with a strong centralized and fully functional government, with an aristocratic elite, and a territorial base of powers. The peasants were made to sustain this government with the sweat of their brow, by producing more crops for their government, before feeding their families. The military force was of both infantry and naval, including the help of Zheng He (1371-1435) and his Great Fleet. A great famine began and flooding in the land devastated the peasant class. The people were forced to make new changes to the technology they used in agriculture, textile production - such as the silk looms and cotton mills, and find new ways of producing the products the government demanded, including paper and ceramics.

There was a great inequality of wealth, status, and livelihoods. Merchants and peasants began to find new ways of making money, including trading with outsiders, especially Europeans. The Dynasty cracked down on the people, considering any unsanctioned trade "piracy,"

creating pirates in China like **Ching Shi**. At this point, there was a great uprising from the Northern clans, made of Manchu, Han, and Mongol elements, who captured Beijing and overthrew the Ming Dynasty (1636), setting up the Qing Dynasty, ruled mostly by Manchus and governed like their predecessor. This was the last Great Imperial Dynasty. Christian missionaries and Jesuits entered China, in 1582, and received an audience with the emperor in 1601. At that point, the Jesuits were taken in by the courts as advisors, for the next 150 years, under both Ming and Qing emperors.

The Rise of Russia – This began as a nomadic area of

many different people. The Slavs of Northern Europe sought refuge in their own land and began construction of two great regions, Moscow and Kiev, in 1240. The Mongols, the Khan, and the Golden Horde, invaded these areas and ruled this province until 1480. In 1462, **Ivan III** was crowned Great Prince, after his father's death, and began taking control of this and many surrounding areas. He began buying and invading many lands, which caught the attention of Khan Ahmed, of the Golden Horde, who demanded tribute to them, of which Ivan defied. The Golden Horde fought back, but could not match Ivan's army and were forced out of Russia. Through invasions and the deaths of his brothers (and inheriting each of their regions), Ivan took over a large portion of modern-day Western Russian, all by 1505. Move forward two generations, and Feodor I the Great invaded more lands to the East, by 1598, and then **Peter the Great** took the rest of the area, to the coast of the Pacific, by 1689. This was a great transition for this region, once ruled by Mongols and later overtaken by Slavs, as they built their nation. Russia, with its Byzantine-influenced culture, became a state of Eastern Orthodox Christian faith after

Ivan III married the niece of the Byzantine Emperor, **Constantine XI**, in 1472. Yet, while the Byzantines ruled much of the Mediterranean, they left the land Northward to the Tsardom dynasty, started by Ivan IV, first Tsar of Russia.

India's Islamic Rule by the Moguls – Conquered in 1206 by the Delhi Sultanate, an Islamic Empire based in Delhi, India was a region with set boundaries, and a people under Islamic rule. They are noted as one of the only Empires to thwart the Mongol invaders and the first and only Muslim Empire to be rules by a woman, Razia Sultana, for four years. They were also known for the destruction and attacks on Hindu and Buddhist structures and gatherings, nearly eradicating these faiths from India. This empire dissolved by 1352, and it was

taken by the Bengal Sultanate, who were also Sunni Muslims. It was under their rule that peasants began to starve. Hindus began to rise and claim regions of Southern India back from the Empire, and started a movement towards Sikhism. In 1526, the Mughal Empire, ruled by Babur, with the help of his neighbors - the Ottomans and Safavid Empires, took over all of India again, overthrowing the Sultan of Delhi. This began the proto-Industrialization period, making India one of the biggest global economies and manufacturing power, around the 1580s. This empire lasted until 1720.

Japan's Development – This was a very turbulent time for Japan, and yet, was part of its developmental stage.

Theirs was a society designed similar to European feudalism. The Ashikaga government preceded the **Kamakura** era. These wars, including the Onin War (1467-77), destroyed Kyoto and so collapsed the shōgunate's power. It was not until 1582 that peace was again established, when the first, Oda Nobunaga, took control of Kyoto and disposed of the Ashikaga shogun.

Activity: Map Making – Much was happening throughout Asia during this time. There were many different rulers than there are today. We want you to map out these different rulers. Their borders are not well defined, and there are no specific countries organized, because this is before the time of defined borders (and the occurrence of constant wars changing the boundaries), but there is a distinction between most of the regions throughout Asia. Go to this site www.HuntThePast.com/AsianRenaissance to get the entire assignment, to map out what was happening in Asia. We will provide you a map of what were the most common borders during this time. Design the map from the printout prepared on the site, and then replicate the map in the space below.

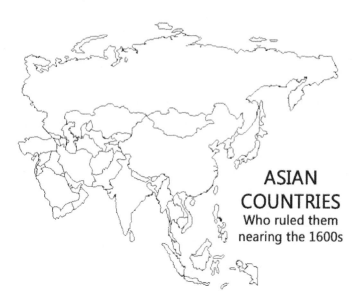

ASIAN
COUNTRIES
Who ruled them
nearing the 1600s

Activity #2: Critical Thinking – The events of one nation almost always influence other nations. How do you think Asian influences affected Europe, and the Age of Exploration? Think of different possibilities of how Europe was affected, including the Spice Trade - and trade all together, wars that may have occurred, diplomacy between nations, and economic struggles that were caused by Asian nations in Europe.

_____

_____

_____

_____

_____

_____

_____

_____

_____

_____

_____

_____

Why would Europe feel that exploration was so important to their survival? Why was the Age of Exploration so important to Europeans?

_____

_____

_____

_____

_____

_____

_____

_____

_____

_____

_____

_____

AFRICA (W4:D3):

Africa in the 1400s – Between 1100 and 1600 AD, "The Golden Age" of trade in Africa, Trans-Saharan Trade was flourishing. African gold was at high demand, and people from around the world came to trade for it. The spread of Islam, throughout Africa, came with much conflict, as the larger Muslim empires would attack a city and then force them to convert. This mostly occurred in Northern Africa and the Eastern Coast. The Nomadic Almohad people invaded Spain in the 11th Century, but between 1482 and 1491, during the Spanish Reconquista, they pushed them out of Spain and back into North Africa.

Mansa Musa (1280-1337) – The tenth Mansa of the Mali

Empire became very well known. The Mali Empire had conquered other African territories in North Africa, such as Ghana, Guinea, and Gambia. He was given the title of "Lord of the Mines of Wangara." His mastery of mining and slave labor helped his expansion of gold production, making him the wealthiest man in history.

He was a devout Muslim, and pushed for full conversion throughout his Empire. His Hajj (or pilgrimage to Mecca), between 1324 and 1325, is legendary, not just in North Africa, but around the world, because of what occurred on his journey. This journey was approximately 2,700 miles and took him almost a year to complete. His entourage included 60,000 men, all wearing expensive clothing, but armed for war; 12,000 slaves, who each carried gold bars and staffs, dressed in silk; and hundreds of horses and camels, to carry enough food for their entire precession. Each camel carried 300 lbs. of gold dust. On his journey, he would give this gold away to the poor throughout Cairo and Medina, and traded some for souvenirs. This large precession made him well known among all of Africa, and the world.

On the way home, Musa discovered the effect of his generosity. He returned only months later, to find that the economies of each of these cities were destroyed. The value of gold, because of this large influx, became almost worthless, for about ten years. The price of food and other goods became extremely high. Some historians believe that on his journey back, he tried to gather as much of the gold as possible, to salvage what he had done; or was this his plan? Others believe that this pilgrimage was not religious, but to get the world's attention and destroy Cairo's market, being the leading gold market at the time. It was only in 1375 that his Empire was finally added to the world maps of his time.

To receive more attention from the world, he enlisted architects from Spain and Cairo to build his grand palace and mosque in Timbuktu. This city became the African center of trade, culture, and Islam. Merchants would bring their greatest trades to this market, and universities were built and staffed with Musa's pick of Astronomers and Mathematicians. Many of these buildings, minus his palace, still stand today.

Trans-Saharan Trade Market – Imagine you were in a land that only produced one or two goods. If you wanted something different, you would need to travel and trade what you had, for what you wanted or needed. Trade in all of Africa was essential and these trade routes began thousands of years BC, until around the 17th century. While some areas had an abundance of gold, others had an abundance of other goods and materials, so tribes would travel the entire continent to find the right market 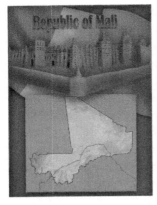 to sell, trade, and buy. There were many different markets you could travel to, but none were as grand as the markets of Mali, for not only were they full of merchants from Africa, but Europe and Asia as well. They all desired different goods and were willing to trade what they had for materials: metals, such as gold and silver; food, from crops to livestock; materials, such as silk and cotton; and even humans (slaves) were high-priced goods in these markets. Slaves would be traded by the hundreds at a time. Not only were these markets to sell goods in, but also markets used for that of teaching and conversion. The Islamic religion and cultures from around the continent were traded. Languages were so different when it all began, and slowly the traders would learn other languages, aside from their native tongue, to work the market. Nothing was held back from being sold in these markets.

Something else to note, is that the Saharan Desert covered a large portion of Northern Africa. So much, that when Europeans and Asian conquerors would attack Africa, they would keep to the Northern coast, because the desert literally covered the northern half from the rest of the continent (which is why you see conquerors clinging to the areas in direct contact with the northern coast of Africa). This was not just because they desired to control the Mediterranean Sea, but also because there wasn't much south of them, before the Sahara devoured everything. Only those brave enough and well equipped could navigate the ever changing sands of this ocean-like area. Traders would come in caravans of camels - animals that could take both the heat and lack of water. Most of the markets lay southeast of the Saharan Desert, or near the coast, where traders were able to have access. Some of the largest markets were accessible by the water, and allowed Europeans to travel there.

African Slavery – Slavery can be found in abundance, throughout all of history, in nearly every country around the world. The ethnicity or race of the slave did not matter, but instead it only mattered that you were weaker than the person taking you into servitude, but strong enough to work. Nowhere else was this in such abundance than in Africa. You were taken into slavery for these main reasons: being captured in war; to pay off your debt; military servitude; prostitution; and criminal

slavery. Indentured servitude was another type of slavery, but was temporary, and as soon as you paid your debt or served your prison sentence, you were to be released. Both slaves and indentured servants were traded at these trans-Saharan markets, as individuals, or by the hundreds. Though it started in Africa, thousands of years before

Europe began to play a big part, the first records were written by the Greek philosopher Herodotus, in the 5th century BC. He argued that slavery was essential for much of these civilizations to survive, and so justified the Greeks to participate. He argued that these people would be forced to create irrigation, harvest crops, and even construct great infrastructure and buildings that could not be done by locals.

One great nation, built on slavery, was that of Cairo, and all of Egypt. They had many eras of slavery with people enslaved from all over Africa. They were consistent procurers of human life and much of the country was built on their backs, including the great pyramids and other architecture throughout the country, and in the deserts. Their slaves would then have children, and they too would be placed into servitude, at an incredibly young age. Though slavery was in abundance in Africa, Romans were the first Europeans to enter the interior of Africa, and purchase slaves near the 5th century BC.

Muslim traders entered the market in the 7th century, yet Islamic law would not allow Muslims to take other pre-existing Muslims as slaves, so most of their captives would come from areas they were conquering. During the Byzantine and Ottoman wars, both Christian and Muslim forces would enslave each other, and add them to their forces, whether to fight or to serve. In the 13th century, an army - called the **Mamaluks** - who were slave

soldiers that converted to Islam, were turned into their own army to take other non-Muslim areas, or used to attack Crusaders on their pilgrimage to Jerusalem. Slavery became so overwhelming in Europe that the Roman Catholic Church banned all slave trade for a short time and then reopened it, prohibiting slaves taken in Christian areas to be sold to non-Christian markets. Jewish merchants specialized in "Pagan Europeans," and shipped them to the African markets.

As European countries entered the slave market, the price of slavery increased dramatically, because of their demand for servants of all types. For this reason, slavery in Africa increased, and those who purchased them would ship them overseas - both to their countries and even to the New World. Europeans, mostly criminals and those who owed a debt, were taken into slavery and shipped to the Americas as well. Between 1500 and 1900, the Barbary Pirates, Muslim privateers of the Mediterranean Sea, were known to have captured over a million white slaves and sold them in African markets. The number of slaves can only be estimated, as no records were kept, but these were more of estimates of the numbers that were needed to replace those slaves who would have died during their servitude. During  this time, it is possible that nearly 17 million slaves were sold in the Indian Ocean, Middle East, and Northern Africa. The number on the West Coast and Cape of Africa are unknown.

Activity: Adobe Castle – Most buildings in Mali were designed and built with brick or wood, and covered with a material called Adobe (mud), to keep the interior cool and moist. Your task today is to design a building in the space below and then to go outside to build it. You may use sand, mud, or any other dirt-like substance, including wet flour, if you need to make your project inside. Draw your structure below, first, and then go to www.HuntThePast.com/Adobe to learn how to build it:

Activity #2: Slavery Experiment (W4:D4) – Today, you will participate in a simple assignment. You will give yourself a small feeling of what being a slave felt like. You will give yourself to another student, or family member, and act as their slave for a day. For this experiment, that person may not hurt you or do anything that you would not do before this activity, much like slaves would experience, but you must serve them the entire day.

What did you feel as a slave for someone else?

_____

_____

Was your captor mean or nice to you, as their slave?

_____

Did they have you do anything you did not want to do?

_____

What were some of the chores you had to do for them?

_____

_____

Actual Slavery: We only gave you a taste of what slavery would have felt like, without the abuse and harsh conditions. Now, reflect on what actual slaves - back a few hundred years ago - would have felt.

How might they have felt, as a slave for someone else?

_____

Did they have them do anything they did not want?

_____

What were some of the responsibilities they had to do?

_____

_____

Conquest of Cuba – During Columbus's first voyage, they left Hispaniola and sailed west to find a large island that they mistook for the mainland of Asia. On his second voyage, they built their first settlement in Cuba, working with the Taino and teaching them their Christian faith. Two years after Columbus's death, in 1508, the entire island was mapped, proving it was not mainland Asia.

In 1511, Diego Velázquez de Cuéllar was ordered by Spain to conquer the island. Hatuey, a Chieftain from Hispaniola, who escaped with 400 Taino in canoes, came and warned the locals about the attack. He then took up arms and conducted guerrilla warfare tactics against Velázquez, taking out 8 Conquistadors before being taken. He was tried and quickly put to death.

Bartolomé de las Casas took part in this assault and later, after giving up slavery, described it as a massacre. In one such battle, he detailed a thousand villagers greeting the Spaniards with loaves and fishes before Velázquez attacked, killing many and sending the rest scattering into the surrounding islands. Most Taino were captured and placed on a reservation. In 1513, Ferdinand II sent out a decree, the **Encomienda**, granting land and slaves to Spaniards who participated.

Velázquez was made governor over Cuba and told to divide the land and the Taino among the Conquistadors, and to govern their use of the land for farming and the search for gold. The Taino resisted and escaped, whenever possible. Hernan Cortez, a young Conquistador, took part in the massacre and was granted land, but saw bigger things for his future.

Activity: Map Making - You just took over Cuba, and now need to divide the island into 10 sections. You are not taking over Taino land but working around them. Find a map of Cuba, and draw it in the space below. Map out five imaginary villages of Taino, drawing small circling to show their land, and then divide the rest into 10 equal parts. Each plot of land must have access to a coast in order to ship the gold they find and crops they grow. How would you divide this island to satisfy both Taino and Spaniards?

Welcome to the Island of Cuba
You are commanded, by the Spanish crown, to divide this island into 10 equal parts. You are allowed to keep the native villages where they are, but you must divide the rest.

Hérnan Cortés (1485-1547) (W5:D2)– Born into a  middle-class military family, he was related to two very influential people in the Americas: maternal cousins with **Francisco Pizarro,** and through his dad, **Nicolás de Ovando,** third governor of Hispaniola. By age 16, he had already returned from university, and with news of Columbus's journey, Cortés was ready to set sail, but was too young.

At 19, he was sent immediately into Cuba to help Cuéllar conquer the island. For his service, he was given an encomienda, land, and Taino servants, to serve in farming and gold exploration. This did not last long, as he became bored with farming, and found no gold. He heard other explorers finding new lands west of Cuba, and desired to do the same, finding his own fortune.

It was not until his thirties that he was given his chance. He was commissioned to sail to the mainland, but his superiors changed their minds and tried to take it away from him. Hearing this, he defied them, and set sail anyway. He had heard of the great city of Tenochtitlan and sought an audience with the Aztec Emperor, Moctezuma. Arriving, he automatically won the favor of local tribes. Those who would not join his expedition willingly, he would fight, and then add them to his army, involuntarily. He came upon the Tlaxcala, archrivals to the Aztec, and went to war; neither side defeated the other, so they decided to talk. Cortés was invited to the city of Tlaxcala by their elder, Xicontenga. There was so much animosity towards the Aztecs that Cortés and Xicontenga became allies.

Cortés traveled next to Tenochtitlan and was invited in, as a guest, by their leader, Moctezuma. He was buying time, because his army was away harvesting. Since the city was in the middle of a lake and Cortés and his men were surrounded by hundreds of thousands of Aztec, Moctezuma thought it was best to keep them close. Cortés, though, had a plan, and he began taking notes of the layout of the city and how to attack. Before he could dispatch his plan, he learned that his superiors had sent an army with **Alonso Álvarez de Piñeda,** from Cuba, to capture him. He rushed back to the coast to defeat the army. Piñeda sent soldiers to land to scope out the area, but before they could attack Cortés, they were surrounded and taken. Piñeda was sent away empty handed. The men Cortés took, joined his army.

When Cortés returned to Tenochtitlan, it was chaos, as the Conquistadors Cortés left had begun a massacre among the Aztec, killing **Moctezuma**. The Aztec forced the Spanish out. Cortés did not stop though, he joined

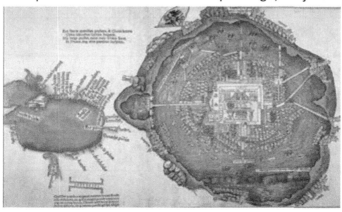

forces with Tlaxcala and attacked Tenochtitlan again, until they submitted. He renamed the land "New Spain," and was made Governor over the entire region. He rebuilt Tenochtitlan and called it Mexico-Tenochtitlan. He continued forward to Honduras and Guatemala, launching him into great debt. He later returned to Spain to live out the rest of his life as a disgruntled old man.

Among Cortes's Conquistadors was **Juan Garrido**, originally from Kongo, Africa. He traveled to Spain as a young man and converted to Christianity, choosing a Spanish name. He became a Spanish soldier to sail with Cortez, and eventually took over Tenochtitlan. His reward was a large plot of land near the city, and he became the first to plant wheat in America.

Activity: Hard Decisions - When arriving in the mainland, Cortés had to rally his men to action, so he destroyed his ships so there was no return. In life, each of us must make hard decisions. Ask you parents what their hardest decision has ever been. Ask them for the entire story and in the space below, give a summary.

_____

_____

_____

_____

_____

Activity #2: Map Making - In the space below, draw a map of your house, and give small descriptions of things around the house - like the picture of Tenochtitlan from a few pages back. If you have a second floor, draw that separately. Add details that you may want to highlight:

Juan Ponce de Leon (1474-1521) (W5:D3) – Born into nobility, Juan started his career at a young age, serving as a squire to a Knight, and a page to the royal courts of Aragon. He began learning warfare and served in the campaign of Spain against Granada, as they defeated the Moors, and the re-establishment of Spain in 1492, just as **Christopher Columbus** was asking the Crown to fund his expedition. With the war won, **King Ferdinand and Queen Isabella** decided to fund Columbus on his voyage. It is believed that because the war was over, there was no need for the number of soldiers, and so they sent them to the new world, including Ponce de Leon.

Years later, he traveled back to Spain and returned with **Nicolás de Ovando,** to take over for Francisco de Bobadilla - enemy of Columbus and friend of Queen Isabella - as he was under investigation for the ill treatment of the indigenous people (and possibly lying to the crown during Columbus's investigation). Francisco was originally sent to Hispaniola as a judge, where he imprisoned Columbus and then shipped him back to Spain for trial. Francisco died on his return to Spain, sunk by a hurricane Columbus predicted (that no one believed).

Ponce de Leon thwarted an overthrow by the Indigenous people on Hispaniola, and Ovando rewarded him with a new governorship, though this was short-lived because of his many power-hungry rivals. When rumors of a large amount of gold on the nearby island of San Juan Bautista (now known as Puerto Rico) reached Ponce de Leon, he left his post to explore the nearby islands. When he realized he needed more funding, he requested that the crown pay for such an adventure. They funded him with supplies, a ship, and 50 men, and he immediately set sail to the island, establishing a new settlement.

While there, he came upon the Bimini people, who spoke of a spring or fountain that would rejuvenate their life, making them young again. This drove Juan to search out more islands of gold, and to begin his search for the Fountain of Youth. He set sail again in 1513, and landed near what is now St. Augustine, Florida, believing it was just another island. He made many different discoveries while exploring, including a gulf stream - a warm body of water moving straight east that Spanish ships could use to quicken their journey back to Spain. Returning to Puerto Rico and then Spain, he reported his finding and was made Governor over Puerto Rico and Florida, and given an army to "protect" them from the local tribes.

When he returned to Florida, near modern day Port Charlotte, it is reported that the indigenous people, the Calusa, attacked his men and settlers and mortally wounded Leon, who was shot in the thigh. His men sailed him back to Cuba, where he soon died.

Activity: Map Making - Where did Juan Ponce de Leon travel? Draw on this map where he would have sailed. Start in Spain, then to Hispaniola, Puerto Rico, St.

Augustine, Puerto Rico, Spain, Port Charlotte, Florida, and Cuba. Chart his travels.

Alonso Álvarez de Piñeda (1494–1520) (W5:D4)– Born in Spain, he studied to be a cartographer, or map maker. When he arrived in the Americas, at age 25, Francisco Garay, Governor of Jamaica, commissioned Alonso to find them a new settlement that had inhabitants who he could use for labor and find a way to reach the Pacific Ocean. Jamaica was crumbling, due to its indigenous

people dying of European diseases, like Smallpox, Influenza, and Measles, and the **Conquistadors**, having nowhere else to explore. Piñeda was obliged to lead Garay's expedition and use his map making skills to find a new land, taking over for Juan Ponce de Leon, and exploring more of Florida, after his passing.

He quickly set sail from Jamaica with three ships, 270 men, and many supplies, up the West coast of Florida. He mapped the coastline and every river that looked like a possible connection to the Pacific, through Alabama, Mississippi, Louisiana, and Texas, which together they claimed for Spain, and named Amichel. Piñeda disproved **Juan Ponce de Leon's** claim that Florida was an island. He took detailed notes on the inhabitants, and even settlements that he encountered as he sailed around the coast. When he reached Texas, he discovered a land full of indigenous inhabitants, of which he named Corpus Christi Bay, after the day he arrived - the Roman Catholic Feast Day of Corpus Christi. Many of his crew wanted to explore Texas, but there are questions if he left the ship and explored with them or not.

They continued their journey into Mexico, down to the area now called Vera Cruz. Before leaving Jamaica, Governor Garay gave Piñeda a secret charge, to intercept **Hérnan Cortés's** flotilla and claim that land for Spain. When they reached Cortés (near modern day Vera Cruz), while sending a landing party to take command, Piñeda's soldiers were captured. This is also when Piñeda found that Cortés was about to attack the Aztec Empire. Alonso was forced to sail back up the coast to Rio Panuco, near modern-day Tampico, and while exploring the river and repairing his ship, was attacked by Huastec Indians. They destroyed everything and killed everyone in his party. Still, somehow, his map made its way back to Garay and, though inaccurate, was used by dozens of future explorers.

Activity: Cartographer – You are now a mapmaker for the day. Go outside and, without using any current maps, design a map on a blank sheet of paper, marking houses and roads, fences, and other structures, including landscaping and any waterways in your neighborhood. Draw it in the space below:

Vasco Nunez de Balboa (1475-1519) (W6:D1)

Born to wealth, Vasco Nunez de Balboa wanted to declare his independence and claim the treasures of the New World, returning one-fifth - called the *Royal Fifth* - to the King. After his first voyage, he took his earnings and retired to Hispaniola, but quickly lost all his money, falling into great debt. He left Hispaniola to distance himself from his debtors, hiding in a barrel, with his dog, aboard a Spanish ship commanded by Martín Fernández de Enciso (whose task was to assist Alonso de Ojeda in securing his fort in Tierra Firme, the Northern half of South America). Balboa was discovered and Enciso threatened to leave him on the next deserted island to die. Thanks to Enciso's crew, and his knowledge of the region, Balboa was spared.

By the time they arrived at the settlement, the war with the local tribe was lost, and the colonists were leaving their fort to return home, with **Francisco Pizarro** and 70 colonists. Balboa talked the captain and Pizarro into resettling in an area called Darién, where they found great opposition. Yet, they still fought and won, taking over the native village when the tribe abandoned it. They named the settlement Santa María la Antigua del Darién. The crew preferred Balboa over their captain, who tried to make himself mayor. They overthrew Enciso, and established the first open government, and a municipal council, electing Balboa to a seat. Nicuesa, Governor of Veragua, a nearby region, became jealous of their success and tried to overthrow Balboa, but his people were loyal to him. Nicuesa and 17 of his men were banished to the sea. Balboa then became Governor of Santa Maria and Veragua.

His first act as Governor was to imprison Enciso and strip him of his properties, although he freed him months later, and sent him back to Hispaniola to live out his life. Balboa, in the meantime, continued to explore new lands, make friends with some tribes, and conquer others. Those that fought him were captured and enslaved. These tribes told tales about another sea and untold wealth; and Balboa set off on another expedition.

Because Enciso had returned to Hispaniola to tell of the confrontation with Balboa, Balboa was not provided any provisions to help in his expedition. He left with less than 190 men. On his journey, he came upon one of the tribes that had fled from the Conquistadors, when Balboa attacked less than a year before. This time, the tribe was ready for Balboa, and yet, still failed to stop him and sp they joined his army, along with many other. Nearing the Pacific, many of his soldiers were exhausted and stayed behind while Balboa, a few Conquistadors, and a large indigenous army continued forward. One morning, he climbed the summit of a mountain, to see the Pacific Ocean for the very first time. A few days later, they arrived, and while wading into the water, Balboa declared the Pacific Ocean under Spanish rule. Two months later, he returned by another route, conquering additional tribes. Spain sent more provisions and with them, a new Governor of Santa Maria. Balboa was arrested, but later allowed to lead one last expedition, which ended in failure. He was captured by Francisco Pizarro and, under the command of Espinosa, executed.

Francisco Pizarro (1478-1541) (W6:D2) – Born into  poverty, Francisco Pizarro was ambitious enough to desire to find his fortunes in the new world. He grew up without an education, and without being able to read. He joined the Spanish military in his early 20s, and set off to the New World with Alonso de Ojeda, another Spanish explorer on his second trip to the New World. Ojeda's first trip was sailing with **Amerigo Vespucci**, finding many islands in the Caribbean and travelling down to Venezuela and Columbia.

Pizarro followed him to Tierra Firme, the Northern half of South America. They were given permission to colonize the Gulf of Urabá, in the area of modern-day Columbia and though they tried to build a settlement, the indigenous opposition, constant attacks, and lack of food thwarted their efforts. Not receiving reinforcements, Ojeda left Pizarro in charge of the colony for 50 days, while he gathered the needed support. After 50 days, without support arriving, Pizarro decided to abandon the fort. Before departing, **Vasco Núñez de Balboa** arrived and helped secure their last two ships, and 70 surviving colonists. Ojeda would later return as a prisoner of one of the first Caribbean pirates, Bernardino de Talavera, who was escaping Hispaniola.

Pizarro joined the fleet of Martín Fernández de Enciso. From there, he joined Balboa on his mission to cross modern-day Panama by foot; this land would later be home to the Panama Canal. Their party was the first Europeans to see the Pacific Ocean from the Americas.

After news spread of cities of gold, like El Dorado, Pizarro teamed up with a priest, Hernando de Luque, and a soldier, **Diego de Almagro**, who agreed to explore and conquer South America and find these cities of gold. The original explorer of the area, Pascual de Andagoya, made contracts with many of the indigenous tribes in South America, and they were the ones that told of rivers flowing with gold. On the first expedition, Pizarro would begin the journey without his two comrades. Almagro would stay behind to find more recruits, joining later, and Luque was to find more funding and provisions for the expedition.

In his first expedition, Pizarro started in Panama, and traveled by ship, and on foot. They traveled down the coast of Columbia, but were forced to turn back due to weather, lack of provisions and food, and constant attacks by the indigenous people. Almagro would lose an eye in one of these attacks, when he was shot with an arrow. The men were nearing the point of mutiny after their last battle, the Battle of Punta Quemada, but Pizarro's silver tongue - and his resolve to return for more conquistadors - settled their fire, and they returned to Panama.

The Governor of Panama, Pedrarias Dávila, was discouraged and did not want Pizarro to head another attempt to conquer the South. Dávila was planning his own expedition to conquer the North. Again, Pizarro and his two companions changed the Governor's mind, and they took off on their second attempt. As they traveled south, Almagro left again, to find more provisions, and then sailed back down, to find Pizarro and his men exhausted from the travel. During this trip, they found natives on rafts, with textiles, ceramics, gold, silver, and emeralds for trade. They took aboard a few of these natives to help interpret for them.

On his third trip back to Panama, this time with proof of gold, Almagro was confronted by the new Governor of Panama, who quickly sent ships to retrieve Pizarro and bring him and his men back to Panama. When they arrived, Pizarro defied them and went back down South. Only 13 men would join him, while the others stayed at the fort in Tafur. Pizarro's two friends, Almagro and Luque, returned again to Panama, to talk the Governor into supporting them. He gave them two ships and 6 months, but told them that they were to return if they couldn't find this gold. In 1528, they finally reached Peru, and viewed the riches of the Tumbes tribe. They were welcomed with open arms. They spent some time with the people, but then decided to return to Panama for their final expedition into Peru. They left two men to learn the customs of the people, and the Chieftain gave them two boys to learn Spanish and Pizarro's customs. These two were to become interpreters for Pizarro.

When the new Governor refused to allow another expedition, Pizarro set sail for Spain to speak to King Charles I himself, accompanied by his two new interpreters, gold, silver, fabrics, ceramics, and llamas - or as Pizarro called them, "little camels." The King was quite impressed and promised support, as he left for Italy. In his stead, Queen Isabel of Portugal named Pizarro as Governor of the New Castille and sent him back with provisions. This new position gave him full power to override the governor of Panama and with 250 men, between Spain and the colonies, he was allowed to return and conquer the area of Peru. He left Spain with three ships, 180 men, and 27 horses; another 130 men joined from the colonies.

In 1531, they left for Tumbes, to find their village destroyed by another tribe. So without a safe place to settle, they continued into the interior and built their first settlement, San Miguel de Piura. They set up a tribute system, like that of the Incas, a *repartimiento*, where tribes would provide them with support from their own crops and riches. The Inca's leader, Atahualpa, refused to pay tribute, seeing less than 200 Conquistadors against his 6,000 man army. Pizarro then attacked the army with his 200 men, 3 rifles, and 2 canons, and conquered the people, taking Atahualpa into custody. They set up a justice system in the colony and, even against Pizarro's wishes, executed Atahualpa for murdering his own brother in contempt against Pizarro. The empire was split; some joined with Pizarro, now with more reinforcements of around 500 Conquistadors, while others fought against Pizarro (but in the end, lost to the Spanish). Within two years, they had taken the entire Incan empire. Both Pizarro - Governor of New Castille, and Almagro - Governor of New Toledo, began to fight over their territory, especially over the city of Cuzco. The brothers of Pizarro attacked and executed Almagro. Pizarro would then bankrupt Almagro II, who would, in turn, sneak into Pizarro's palace and assassinate him, with the help of only 20 men.

The greed and power of men had seen the best of Pizarro, his men, and even his friends. It could also be said that the man who "Live(d) by the sword, die(d) by the sword."

Activity: Conquering your Bedroom – Some of you have clean rooms; some have very messy ones. Today, you are to clean your room, and report back what you find. Even the cleanest of rooms has something to explore: a backpack, a drawer, or you may have to clean some other room in your house. Your objective in this activity is to draw the room you choose to clean and catalog the content as you clean it, then report back what you find. First, map the room, by drawing it from a birds eye view. Then number where items are that you find, and describe them below:

Items you find in the room:
1. What items did you find?

_____

Did you know that it was there?

_____

2. What items did you find?

_____

Did you know that it was there?

_____

3. What items did you find?

_____

Did you know that it was there?

_____

4. What did you find in the cleaning of this room, besides items? Was there something you learned about yourself, and can you take from this thing you learned, and make it better?

_____

_____

_____

Ferdinand Magellan (1480-1521) (W6:D3)– Born into Portuguese nobility, Magellan became a page to Queen Eleanor. By the age of 25, he was ready for a new career in exploration and merchantry.  He joined a fleet heading to India, and spent nearly 8 years fighting in many naval battles, including against the Sultans of Gujarat and Egypt. He then traveled with his cousin, Francisco Serrão, to the Portuguese Embassy in Malacca, until conspiracies arose. For their safety, they disembarked from the city-state.

After that, the cousins parted ways. Magellan was promoted, returning to Portugal, and Serrão left for the Spice Islands, to advise the Sultan. Due to false claims made against Magellan, and some vacation that was not authorized, his promotion and employment was terminated. He moved to Spain and married, having two children, but only a few years later, they had all died.

During this sad time in his life, he devoted his time to cartography, the study of map making. He wanted to go back to the Spice Islands, but King Manuel of Portugal denied his request continuously. So, he turned to the new King of Spain, who was given permission by the Pope to explore the Americas, under the Treaty of Tordesillas. King Charles I gave him 5 ships, 270 men, and enough provisions for 2 years on the open sea.

Setting sail on September 20, 1519, and arriving - in what is now Brazil - in December, they continued down the coast moving south. Thinking they may have to travel through the continent, they searched for 3 months for any river that would allow them access to the Pacific Ocean. They made landfall near Rio de Janeiro. The weather was getting too rough, and they needed a place to wait out the winter. Some of his crew turned mutinous, started by three of his four captains who questioned Magellan's abilities and tactics. These captains were killed during and after the struggle, and the lower conspirators were put into bondage. During that winter, one ship was lost, but its crew survived.

They started their journey again, with only 4 ships, in October of 1520 – the Southern Hemisphere's summer season. Within a few days, they reached a bay that led them to what is now known as the Straits of Magellan, at the very southern tip of South America. At this point, one of his ships abandoned the effort and sailed back to Spain. The remaining three entered the Strait and found the Pacific Ocean, near the end of November 1520. Believing the journey would take only a matter of days or weeks, it actually took 3 months and 21 days - and 30 men died of scurvy and starvation.

They made landfall in Guam first, where they were given supplies by the indigenous people. Villagers came aboard and took knives, rigging, and nets, in exchange for the supplies, but the Spanish took this as theft, and sent a raiding party into their village to retrieve the supplies that were stolen. Villagers were killed, and huts burned. This miscommunication made them leave the island quickly, and head towards the Philippines. Here, Magellan befriended many of the local leaders and sent missionaries to teach the people. Many converted, but the island of Mactan resisted and the Spanish became forceful, which started a battle. Though the Spanish were well trained, the Mactan were more in number, and many Spaniards were killed - including Magellan.

Activity #2, Part #1: Map Making – Below is a map of the world. Your job is to chart a path to travel around the world. Unlike Magellan, you will know the world map and where you can stop for supplies. Magellan, on the other hand, had to experience his travels as if blindfolded. To experience this blindness, place your pen on the coast of Spain. Take a piece of paper and cover the rest of the globe, west of Spain. As you move the paper left, chart the path you would sail. This is the path you would travel, being ignorant of where you would make land. When you reach the furthest point to the left of the map, move your pen to the far right of the map, about where you would have ended your journey - on the left side of the map - and put the same piece of paper over the rest of the map. Move the paper as you draw your line across the Pacific Ocean and back to Spain. **Part #2:** Now, without the blindfold, chart a journey that would make the most sense to you, if you were to travel around the world. Stay close to land when possible, so you can pick up supplies. Use two different colored pens to chart these two directions.

Part #3: Was it hard to chart the map when you were blindfolded? What do you think Magellan would have experienced?

_____

_____

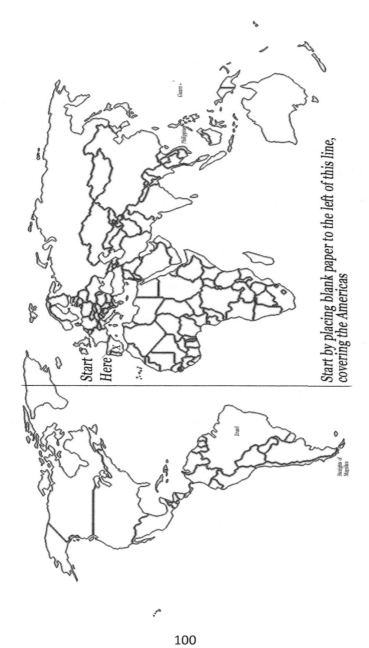

Start Here

Start by placing blank paper to the left of this line, covering the Americas

Guam

Philippines

Brazil

Straights of Magellan

100

BRITISH EXPLORATION OF "AMERICA" (W7:D1)

John Cabot (1450 - 1500) – The greatest geopolitical  issue of these days was trade; to be more specific, the Spice Trade between Europe and Asia. While some controlled the Mediterranean Sea, others, such as Portugal, had permission by the Pope to explore the southern hemisphere, including Africa, and the ability to navigate around its most southern cape and into the Indian Ocean (where they would find their way to India, China, and Indonesia). This brought them many riches, but it also took a very long time traveling there and back. So, some traveled south around Africa, and others west, towards a New World. Cabot, a Venetian, was able to sail throughout the Mediterranean and visit parts of the Middle East, trading with very experienced merchants.

Born Giovanni Caboto in Italy, either from Genoa (like Columbus), or Venice, he was made a citizen of Venice at age 16. Due to this citizenship and high status, he was given the opportunity for maritime trade, including meeting with the Sultan of Egypt, who controlled most trade within Israel, Syria, and Lebanon. Later, he even claimed he had accompanied the Sultan on his visit to the Islamic city of Mecca. During this time, he worked as a merchant, selling and trading for spices and silks. In 1480, while living in Italy, he fell into deep debt; so, he moved to Spain and changed his name, to avoid his debtors. It didn't take long before they found him, and tried to have him arrested. He then moved to Seville, Spain, and asked the crown to attempt an Atlantic expedition. When that failed, he moved to London.

Most explorers who crossed the Atlantic presented their idea to that country's crown and, if accepted, were rewarded with a patent for their idea. Most Spanish ships sailed across the Atlantic, near the equator, where **Christopher Columbus** had sailed, but that journey took a very long time, as the two continents were so far apart. Cabot desired to travel the northern route, thinking that the American continent must be much closer, and his travels much shorter, as he would be closer to the northern pole. This proposal was presented to him by an Augustinian friar, much like how Columbus received the idea he presented to the King and Queen of Spain. The friar then introduced Cabot to the King of England, **Henry VII**. With the tails of Columbus's success spreading throughout Europe, the king accepted Cabot's proposal, and allowed him to sail west to find a faster route.

Note: The Catholic Church funded most universities and scientific exploration during the Renaissance. A myth is that the church was against science, but instead, facilitated most of it, including **Galileo Galilei**, the father of Astronomy; **Nicolas Copernicus**, with his Heliocentric Solar System; **Georges Lemaître**, who first theorized the big bang theory; **Louis Pasteur**, and his discovery of vaccinations. It is no wonder why both Columbus and Cabot would have received these ideas of  traveling west from friars who studied science and theorized that the earth was round, not flat, like others.

Now just because the king accepted Cabot's patent does not mean that he gave Cabot funding or any vessels to explore the new world. Instead, he merely allowed him to sail there under the English flag. Though the Pope had issued the Treaty of Tordesillas, giving the Spanish the Americas and Portugal Africa and Asia, the King of England, a practicing Catholic, decided to send his own expedition and claim part of the New World for his crown. So, in this sense, the King of England was giving Spanish -financed Columbus some competition. Cabot finished finding financing for this trip - which he would have to pay back through treasures from the New World - and set sail across the Atlantic. Soon the weather turned on him, and he was forced to return.

He was better known for his second attempt, even though neither journey was well documented, (only a few letters, and an article in the Bristol Chronicle, where he set sail). Note: while Columbus was a passionate writer, and also had others record his success, Cabot was not, and did not have scribes among his sailors. Most sailors at the time were illiterate, or without the needed time to put their thoughts to paper. It is said that he left with a small vessel, 8 months of provisions, and only about 20 men, including William Weston - the first Englishman to lead an expedition to North America.

Where he landed is not certain, but Canada has now deemed **Cape Bonavista** to be the official landing place. He did not explore much beyond the shoreline, but took time to claim the land for the King of England and the Roman Catholic Church, take on fresh water, and quickly explore the coast, before heading home. Cabot reported back to the king and was given a cash award that was equivalent to 2 years pay for a laborer (and twice that as a yearly salary), but Cabot only wanted the recognition of his importance. In 1498, he set sail on his final voyage, this time with five ships. There are no other records of Cabot and any future expedition. It is said that he was lost at sea, either sailing to the New World, or returning. The friars who came on this expedition are believed to have started a mission in Newfoundland. William Weston led his first expedition to the New World in 1499.

Activity: Map Making – To better understand exploration of the New World, let us map out the voyages of the map makers, by drawing out their expeditions: where they may have set sail from, and where they may have landed. This will take additional research. Find the sailing routes of Leif Erickson, Christopher Columbus, John Cabot, Ferdinand Magellan, and at least two other explorers (including Amerigo Vespucci, Hernan Cortez, Francisco Pizarro, Vasco Nunez de Balboa, Juan Ponce de Leon, and/or Alonso Álvarez de Piñeda). It is understood that a lot of Spanish explorers took similar routes, but try to make it look as legible and organized as possible when you draw it:

Question: Does drawing each of their voyages help you understand the exploration of the Americas?

Sir Walter Raleigh (1552 - 1618) and the Lost Colony of Roanoke (1587) (W7:D2) - The outer banks of North Carolina was explored by Giovanni da Verrazzano, in 1524, who promptly returned to Francis I, King of France, and Henry VIII, King of England, to report a route to China; though, with additional exploration, he would have seen that it was only a barrier island, protecting the mainland. In their wisdom, neither Kings granted further exploration.

In 1578, Queen Elizabeth I commissioned Sir Humphrey Gilbert to explore the east coast of the New World (that not already claimed by any Christian nation - Florida was already claimed by Spain). Gilbert died in 1584, and his commission was split between his brother, Adrian Gilbert, and half-brother, Walter Raleigh. They were to claim the east coast, with Raleigh given the southern portion to explore and settle by 1591, or lose his rights.

Raleigh had found favor with the queen, by playing a major role in colonizing and thwarting the rebellions in Ireland. For his part, he was given a portion of Ireland to farm and mine. His influence grew, by serving the queen under many positions, including helping her to thwart the Spanish Armada's attempts on **Britannia**.

In his commission, he was to colonize Virginia, search for gold, and set up a base for privateers - legal pirates commissioned to attack Spanish treasure ships. Now Raleigh never landed in, or explored, North America; he delegated that responsibility to others. Instead, he and his friends sailed off to search for El Dorado, the city of gold, in what is now known as Venezuela, and returned to publish a book about the city- which was debunked.

His first colony was founded in Virginia, on Roanoke Island. The first expedition was unfruitful, so he sent a second one, with a larger group of settlers. When they landed, they began to span out across Roanoke Island. They were well supplied and very driven to settle the land. They were governed by John White, who,  when their supplies were running out, decided to return to England for more. His return was delayed, first, by all ships being recalled to help fight the Spanish Armada, and then further delayed when his fleet was sidetracked by the thought of attacking Spanish treasure ships.

When White arrived, the colony had disappeared. The settlers may have given up and moved, writing "CRO" into the trunk of a tree. "CRO" could have meant they moved to Croatoan Island, off North Carolina, but due to bad weather, White was never able to find them.

As for Raleigh, he secretly married one of the Queen's ladies-in-waiting, in 1591, and when discovered, in 1592, he and his new wife were locked in the Tower of London. He was temporarily released, a month later, to help manage the return of privateer vessels recalled by the queen. After his full release in 1593, he became part of Parliament. After the Queen died, he was accused of treason against **King James I,** and sent back to the tower. In 1617, he was granted another pardon and received a commission to peacefully search for El Dorado again. But, unbeknownst to him, one of his vessels broke a peace treaty, and attacked a Spanish outpost. Raleigh's son was killed. Raleigh returned to Spain and, though given opportunities to escape, he accepted his execution. His wife was presented with his head, and kept it until her death.

Activity: Storytelling of the Past – Your task is to create a story of what you think happened to Roanoke. Why did the settlers leave; or was the colony destroyed with them inside? You have free rein over this story. You can make it what you actually believe happened to the city, or what most likely didn't happen, but could have – try to be realistic. How do you see an entire colony disappearing? Read the unit on the Lost Colony of Roanoke at HuntThePast.com. Write your story first on a separate sheet of paper, and then condense it to fit in the space below.

_____

_____

_____

_____

_____

_____

_____

_____

James VI of Scotland and I of England (1566 – 1625)
Childhood (W7:D3): Every family is different, and some have more apparent problems than others - issues that are seen by the public eye, and some that are not. You may have a family that struggles; King James I, though royalty, had a very difficult family and childhood.

He was the son of Mary, Queen of Scots (Scotland), and Henry Stuart, Lord Damley; they were both grandchildren to Margaret Tudor, daughter of Henry VII, and sister of Henry VIII. Now, because they were born and ruled in different kingdoms, Henry VIII was of the House of Tudor, while James VI was of the house of Stewart; when his cousin, twice removed, died, he ascended from one throne to two thrones. Did you get all that? At his birth, England and Scotland were split kingdoms, and James's ascension to the English throne brought them together, to be ruled under one crown.

Now James VI's parents were both Roman Catholic, but as the Protestant population grew, it strained the kingdom - and the marriage - of these two monarchs. In 1566, his father even plotted with the Protestants to murder Mary's private secretary, because of infidelity, just before James was born. This act nearly ripped the country in two, and was the demise of Mary's reign.

Three months after the murder, on June 19, 1566, James was born. Five days later, he was baptized as "James Charles," Duke of Rothesay and Prince and Great Steward of Scotland. Less than one year later, his father, Damley, was murdered, and James inherited his father's title, Duke of Albany. Three months later, Mary married James Hepburn, 4th Earl of Bothwell, who was suspected of murdering her husband, as revenge for murdering her private secretary. For these acts, and others, a group of Protestants kidnapped and imprisoned the queen in Loch Leven Castle, where she was never to see her son again. She was forced to abdicate her throne to her infant son, on July 24, 1567. Mary's half-brother, James Stewart, Earl of Moray, as regent, was to care for the throne until James was old enough to do so. In 1568, Mary escaped and gathered her troops to attack Stewart. She lost, forcing her to escape to England, where she was captured by Queen Elizabeth, her sister. Stewart was assassinated in 1570, and the regency was given to three others, who were murdered in different ways, all before James reached the age of adulthood, 13, and took the throne, in 1579. FYI, his last regent was executed in 1582, in connection with the murder of James's father. James was raised a Protestant, as were most Scottish nobles.

Early Adulthood: Now jump forward a little, for the next few years are full of James being locked in a tower, and being blasted from the pulpit by priests he put in charge, cursing him for his horrible behavior. His finances were an absolute mess; he was a rebellious and irresponsible adolescent, who was given a throne and great responsibility at a very young age.

In 1586, he signed a treaty with his neighboring kingdom of England, also ruled by distant relatives, and the next year his mother was executed. It is said that all these things needed to happen for him to receive the English crown from Queen Elizabeth when she died. She, on the other hand, paid him to gain influence over the Scottish crown. He even supported her efforts during the 1588 **Spanish Armada** wars.

As part of his plan to take England, he married Anne of Denmark; her father was Fredrick II, Protestant King of Denmark. As she traveled to him by sea, a storm forced her ship to turn around. James, desiring to see and marry her, took his own ships to bring her to Scotland. They were married on November 23, 1589. Historians record their endearing love for each other. They had three children, who survived to adulthood.

Now before much of this nobility took power in England, Wales, Ireland, and Scotland, the land was full of pagans, spanning from the Celtics to the Anglo-Saxons. When Roman Catholic monarchs took over, they desired to push out the pagan faiths, and witchcraft became commonplace. For this reason, the Witchcraft Act of 1563 was enforced throughout the kingdoms. James became interested in these witch hunts, spanning from his in-law's kingdoms to his own. He wrote about it quite extensively, and that writing supposedly helped impact Shakespeare to write the *Tragedy of MacBeth*.

While King of Scotland, James VI also fought to unite the islands west of Scotland, and forcibly dissolve their kingdoms. Believing that they were "barbarians," he sent colonists to take over the land, and set up their own settlements throughout the isles. While the local forces kept them out for a while, the colonists continued until successful. Remember that most of these kingdoms were owned by James's distant relatives, and if they resisted, they were imprisoned or executed.

Ascension to the Throne: In 1601, Queen Elizabeth was notably dying, and knowing that James VI was to ascend the throne, they began a campaign to show the world that he was the natural successor. On March 24, 1603, Queen Elizabeth died, and James made his way south to take the throne, arriving in London only 9 days after her funeral, on May 7th. There was no uprising or invasion, as some had feared; it was a smooth transition. His coronation was on July 25th, making him now James I, King of England. But, due to the plague spreading through the land, the planned festivities were canceled. This did not, however, stop the men and women of England from coming out and celebrating the new King and Queen.

The kingdom came with many issues: the government's taxation of the people was strangling commerce and the livelihood of its people; the corporations were given too many favors, and were monopolizing the smaller businesses; and because of a war with Ireland, they were massively in debt. Though people were hoping for change, those who secretly prepared James I for his throne in 1601 were also kept in power, though James I added some of his own trusted advisors. This included many noblemen from Scotland, to help him unite the two kingdoms, which was one of his highest priorities. In his first year, James I survived two plots to take his throne, the most notable by **Sir Walter Raleigh**, the man who unsuccessfully settled the colony on Roanoke Island.

His desire to unite the kingdoms was fought by both Parliaments. After being denied the title "King of Great Britain," he forcibly assumed it, and forced Scotland to accept it, though England would not. He did find more success in his foreign policy, as he worked to end the Anglo-Spanish War and sign a peace treaty with Spain. This included the possibilities of privateering British vessels to take Spanish vessels on the open water, or fight the Spanish colonies in the Americas. With that treaty, came the freedom of Catholic worship again in

England, though oppression continued. A plot was set forth by Catholic rebels to blow up Parliament, from the cellar beneath, which was full of barrels of gunpowder. One rebel, **Guy Fawkes**, was caught, as if he was to set off the explosion, but it is unknown his exact role, because he died denying involvement.

James I and England's struggles continued to grow well beyond the debt, now, as the inflation of the value of their money was growing. Their money was not worth much, and so food was becoming more expensive every day. When Parliament would not grant him the money he required, especially to pay off his debts, he first sent politicians. Then, when Parliament was taking too long, he dismissed them all. He gathered a new Parliament, and after 9 weeks, dismissed them, as well, due to nothing being resolved, and him not getting the funding he desired. He then began to rule without a Parliament, but instead used corporate leaders who could raise money and provide him with what he needed. James also continued to try to strengthen his connection with Spain, by offering Charles, Prince of Wales, to marry Infanta Maria Anna of Spain, which the Catholics loved.

Sir Walter Raleigh was imprisoned multiple times, from 1591, until his full release, in 1617. He was finally released and paid to search for gold in South America. He was given strict instructions not to engage the Spanish, due to their treaty. His expedition was an utter disaster, as one of his ships attacked a Spanish fort. During the battle, Raleigh's son was killed, and Raleigh was sent back to be executed, to appease the Spanish for this mistrust of their treaty. Though given chances, Raleigh would not escape imprisonment. Relations also soured when the Spanish attacked James I's son-in-law, in Bohemia, of which James I called a Parliament to help fund troops to support his son-in-law. With a Parliament again in session, they called for all-out war on Spain, to refill their finances, remembering the income that came from attacking Spanish treasure ships full of gold. They didn't stop there; they desired to end the courtship of Charles, wanting him to marry a Protestant, and reinstate the anti-Catholic laws. They fought over this for days, and Parliament wrote up a petition for their freedom of speech, which James I quickly ripped up, and then dissolved Parliament once again.

By night, Charles traveled to Spain to win favor with his betrothed. She ended up detesting him, and sent him home. With this insult, he - and those he had influence over - called to end the treaty with Spain, and increase the anti-Catholic policies. They forced James I to open Parliament, once again, and the sentiment grew. He was not only struggling with Catholics, but also the Puritans, as they were pulling him in the opposite direction; he would not have it. He began to fight them and many were forced to leave England, along with their riches and taxes they would have paid. To quell this rebellion, he agreed to a few of their demands, including the creation of an English translated Bible, with books that were not the same as the Catholic church. In 1604, he authorized the

translation and publishing of the King James Version of the Bible, which excluded the apocrypha.

English Puritans decided to set sail and settle in the New World, namely Jamestown, with the London Company in 1607, at Culper's Cove in 1610, and Plymouth, outside of Cape Cod, in 1620. Though they were given patents by the king to settle the area just east of the Hudson, they found a better location, unclaimed by the British, and so claimed Plymouth for their faith. From there, Puritans spread to other colonies throughout North America, including the Bahamas, and anywhere they weren't threatened by the King or Catholic rule.

England and Spain again returned to fighting, and privateering was again legalized against the Spanish treasure ships sailing from the new world. Though James I fought almost his entire life to bring the countries together, those also in power were fighting against him. James was racked with disease, arthritis, gout, and kidney stones, due to his heavy drinking. He finally succumbed to his ailments and died, in 1625.

Activity: Genealogy of History - The next four days will be an exploration into your understanding of history, and how one event or person can affect so much throughout history. To accomplish this assignment, you will need to visit: huntthepast.com/genealogy-of-history -real-life-video-game-activities/. Read the introduction, and complete Activity #1. This is an experience you may really enjoy, because we take you through what makes history, and what is affected by history. After you are done with the activity, transfer your two favorite genealogical maps below.

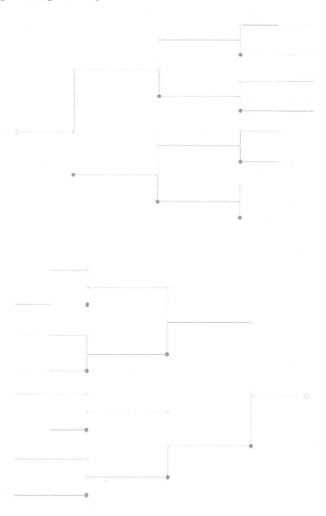

Jamestown (1607) (W8:D1)

Though **Sir Walter Raleigh** failed to establish Roanoke as the first English settlement, **James I, King of England** was set on creating the first settlement and laying claim to part of the New World. For this, he commissioned the London Company to sail to the Americas and establish a settlement, and was willing to do everything in his power to keep it. In 1606, under the command of Christopher Newport, they set sail with three ships: The Discovery, Godspeed, and Susan Constant. On the way, they stopped in the Canary Islands, Puerto Rico, and then sailed north to Cape Henry of Chesapeake Bay, on April 26, 1607. Because of the experiences of the past, and stories of the indigenous people who lived in the New World, they spent days looking for the most secure location, settling on a Peninsula separated from the mainland by a river they called the James River, after the King. The local tribes would not live there, because it was swampy, with too many mosquitos, and poor soils, but the colonists held security as priority over the possibility of crops, as they were first worried of being attacked. For this reason, they spent much of their time preparing a fort, instead of crops. They called it James Fort, again, after the King.

The settlers arrived too late in the season to plant crops, and since most of the settlers were noblemen, they (nor their manservants) knew how to farm. Two-thirds of the settlers died before supplies could reach them in 1608. This was later deemed "Starving Time." To pay for supplies and help from England, those who survived produced materials in James Fort, including wood planks. With the new arrivals came craftsmen and glassmakers; glass became an acceptable product to ship. Because supplies were needed to sustain the first settlers, Captain Newport's second shipment of settlers only added to their starvation. They struggled to irrigate and plant enough crops to sustain the new arrivals. Some of the settlers even went so far as to defect and join the Powhatan tribe, bringing with them weapons and tools; before this, the tribe had none made of iron.

In 1609, the Spanish arrived to scout the area, and were fought off on the sea. The Spanish ship, La Asunción de Cristo, was sent to spy on the settlement, to see if the fort was weak enough to attack, but thanks to the *Mary and John* English vessel, they were kept away.

The London Company's investors wanted more than meager glassware and wood; they were looking for specific items, such as gold, or a survivor from Roanoke. Captain John Smith set out with a small group to explore the area and was attacked by a native hunting party, who killed everyone except Smith. They dragged him through the village, parading him as their trophy. When they were done with him, they laid his head against a rock and when they were to *"beat out [my] brains,"* as Smith

wrote in a letter to the queen, 10-year old Matoaka, daughter of Chief Wahunsenacawh, came to his rescue. When the Chief took over the tribe, he was given the same name as his tribe, Powhatan. Matoaka was given the name **Pocahontas.** She intervened, by cradling his head on her lap, signaling to the rest of the tribe that he wasn't to be feared or killed. It was there that she pleaded for his life. She would also play a pivotal part for the survival of future colonists. Over her early life, she would bring food, and a peace treaty, among her people and settlers.

In 1609, John Smith *was* burned from an explosion during a trade expedition, and was sent back to England to give the bad news about the settlement. He reported that there was not much they could send and no gold to mine, unless they sent more craftsmen who could help them, and would not defect to the local tribes. The London Company got the message, and the third supply run came back with better equipment and supplies.

On the way back, though, a strong storm separated the ships; some of the ships made it to James Fort, but the largest, *the Venture*, carrying most of the supplies, was beached on a reef in the Bahamas. It took the company nine months to build two new ships - the *Deliverance* and the *Patience* - with enough space for all the settlers and supplies, before sailing to James Fort. Those in James Fort were much worse; starvation sent them to harvest every creature in the area, including snakes, and then, when that ran out, they began boiling their leather shoes for subsistence. Only 60 of the 214 original settlers survived. The *Deliverance* and *Patience* arrived in May, 1610, and the survivors were nursed back to health. Deciding the fort was unviable, the survivors boarded the ships and headed back to England. In the meantime, another ship was coming with much needed supplies, and the settlers returned.

With this fourth supply ship came settlers, who demanded much from Chief Powhatan's tribe, and the relationship between the two soured, starting the Anglo-Powhatan War. It persisted until Samuel Argall, a naval officer, captured Pocahontas, who was delivered to him by other tribal leaders. This infuriated Powhatan, but she soon soothed the anger on both sides and helped the settlers negotiate peace. At one point, the Powhatan were to attack the settlers, but again she held them back.

It was the arrival of **Governor Sir Thomas Dale** that changed everything. Until that point, the London Company organized the settlers to farm together and put all crops into a communal storage, and everyone would take what they needed. It was Governor Dale that saw this was not the most effective way to survive. Without permission of the company, he plotted 3-acre farms for each of the original settlers, and smaller plots for the newcomers. They would work the land with their families, and bring their crops to a marketplace, where everyone could purchase and trade crops, according to their wants and needs. The harder the people worked, the better their crops would turn out, and the more they would have (those who couldn't work were supported).

While shipwrecked in the Caribbean, John Ralfe cultivated enough seed of naturally grown tobacco that he could plant it, when he arrived in Jamestown. He was the first successful tobacco farmer in the Americas. Being successful and wealthy, he was given permission to marry the Powhatan chief's daughter, Pocahontas. This brought peace to the colony for some time. In 1616, he and Pocahontas traveled back to England to visit his home. In 1617, she fell ill and died; soon to follow was her father. Pocahontas's brother, a fierce warrior by the name of Opechancanough, was placed in command of the tribe. The settlers encroached more and more into his land to farm, and this again brought contention.

Because of the success of the James Fort, now being called Jamestown, settlers would do anything to leave the starvation and lower-class poverty in England. Since it was so expensive to travel to the American Continent, including room, board, lodging, and land in the Americas, they would register for Indentured Servitude. This meant someone in the Americas would pay their travel expenses, and they, in return, would come serve their benefactors for a specific number of years, (normally three to seven), until they paid back their debt. Those in England who could not pay their taxes, or committed other crimes, would also be stripped of all they owned in England, and sold into servitude, until their debts were paid off. In Virginia, it was against the law to have slaves, but servitude was acceptable. After the debt was paid, they were to receive a portion of their employer's land.

In 1619, the English landowners gathered and organized the first Representative Assembly in America, called the House of Burgesses, to govern everything that happened in the colony. Only English men were to vote, though. This set off the men of other nationalities, who were most of the craftsmen. The Polish artisans held a strike. They demanded they had a vote, or they would not work; and so, they were given the right to equal votes. This assembly's first act was to transfer the land given to settlers to now be owned by their occupants. England and the London Company were no longer owners.

During this same year, the first African slave ship, the *White Lyon*, arrived in Virginia, and sold a family,

Anthony and Isabella Tucker, into indentured servitude. By the time they had their first child, William, they were no longer servants, but landowners. See, the Virginia General Assembly made no distinction between black and white indentured servants, and ended their employment with land and the same privileges. The Spanish and British colonies in the Caribbean and South America differed. Slavery was allowed, and as the farmers relied more on African slavery, the majority race in the Caribbean became of African descent.

NOTE: The first slave owner, in the eyes of an American court, was Anthony Johnson, a man who came to the colonies as an African indentured servant, who bought five of his own servants to plant his 250-acre farm, and their son's 550-acre farms. Anthony's family became very wealthy and influential in Virginia; his wife and daughters were provided the same privileges as white women. In 1653, John Casor, one of his African servants, went to the authorities and claimed that his servitude had expired 7 years previous, but Johnson would not release him and give him his due. Robert Parker convinced Johnson to free Casor and then offered Casor employment on his farm. Johnson sued, in Virginia courts, to keep his servant, and while Casor initially won the case, Johnson appealed and was awarded that Casor was to be returned, and become indentured for life. Though Casor had two white farmers witnessing on his behalf, the precedent of the lawsuit was poorly managed and fought, and that is what lost him the case. In 1655, Casor was the first, in the colonies, to be recognized by the courts as indentured for life, without committing a criminal act. There were many cases of lifetime indentured servants that were awarded because of crimes committed, for both whites and blacks. One such act included running away from legal servitude. The first on record was John Punch, when he, an African servant, and two other white servants tried to escape, and were caught. They were sentenced to lifetime servitude to their employer.

In 1622, the Powhatan could not allow the settlers to take any more of their land, and joined all their forces together. On the morning of March 22, 1622, they attacked, killing everyone in the farms around the outer edge of Jamestown. Even Governor Dale's property, a school developed to teach the indigenous children alongside the colonial children, was destroyed, and 71 attendees and staff were killed. In the end of this surprise attack, 400 colonists were killed, and 40 women were taken captive to serve the Indian tribe, or be ransomed back. The warriors withdrew, believing that the settlers would act like other native tribes and move when they lost, but instead, the colonists planned out their revenge, and a rescue. They wanted to retaliate, but those who were left were women, children, and the elderly - those who could not fight back; so, they laid out a new plan. They released a prisoner to the tribe, to negotiate a peace treaty and the release of the women settlers they had taken. A group of settlers came unarmed to meet with the tribe. As a gesture of good faith, they gave a toast with the Powhatan leaders and warriors, but unbeknownst to the tribe, the wine was poisoned, and 200 of their men and leaders were killed (except Opechancanough, who escaped). Thinking they would be attacked, the Powhatan fled with their women captives. By 1624, 3,400 out of the 6,000 who settled there survived.

Activity: Harvesting - You have come to a new land. You are unfamiliar with the surroundings and the people already living there. What do you do to survive? It is recommended to seek three things: food, shelter, and fresh water. After those are found, the next step is to sustain yourself in the area in which you live. This means that you need to provide a sustainable crop of food for your survival. Have you ever planted a seed and watched it grow? Today, we are going to help you grow your first plant, as if you were a settler planting your first crop. Now they would create fields of these seeds, spaced every few inches, but we are only going to plant one this time. Go to www.huntthepast.com/crops/ to see how to plant your very first seed, and then we'll learn about what it takes to grow those seeds.

Step 2: Now that you have planted the seed, observe its growth and draw what you see:

Week #2 (After 7 days)	Week #2 (After 14 days)	Week #3 (After 21 Days)
Date:	Date:	Date:

What are your thoughts on what you observed?

_____

_____

_____

Pocahontas (1595/1596 – 1617) (W8:D2)

Have you ever written in a journal or kept a record of your early years? Has your mom or dad written down their early memories of you in a journal? Well, the indigenous people throughout the Americas did not. Most of their history and culture was passed down in storytelling, put to memory by one of their tribal members. Because of this, much of Pocahontas's birth and early years is unknown. For the Europeans, on the other hand, many were illiterate, while others were journal keepers and great writers. Most of the stories they have were written down in journals, and that is how we have the history of those people today. Because of these writings, much of Pocahontas's later history is well known around the world - not just in the United States, but all of America and England, where she spent her last few years. And in every journal, she was seen as a savior to the colonists.

When she was born, her father, Chief Wahunsenacawh (also known by the name of his tribe Powhatan), was already in charge of an alliance with 30 Algonquian-speaking nations. Her mother was the first wife of the Chief, but not much else is known. This is because, according to their culture, once one of the Chief's wives gave birth, she was to be returned to her nation, and play little to no place in the child's life. She was then supported until she could be married again. Another possibility is that she died during childbirth.

Pocahontas's mother was not well known among the Europeans, so no record was kept. Pocahontas was not her given name, but a nickname that means "little wanton" or "playful one." She is said to have played, at a young age, with the boys of Jamestown, teaching them how to cartwheel.

Her brother, Opechancanough, was a great warrior and frequently led hunting expeditions. On one of these expeditions, he came upon **Captain John Smith,** and others accompanying his expedition inland. Opechancanough and others attacked the English expedition and killed everyone except John Smith; they had other plans for him. He was to be their trophy. He was led in parade style through the villages as Opechancanough's prisoner, and led to the Powhatan capital of Werowocomoco. When they were done parading him around, they were to execute him in public fashion. Smith reported in his general history that "[they] laid hands on him, dragged him to them, and thereon laid his head, and being ready with their clubs to beat out [my] brains, Pocahontas, the King's dearest daughter, when no entreaty could prevail, got his head in her arms, and laid her own upon his to save him from death: whereat the Emperor was contented he should live."

The Powhatans began to deeply respect the settlers, and considered John Smith a friend to the tribe. Relations were getting better - thanks to Pocahontas's intervention. During a trading expedition, an explosion occurred, and John Smith was severely burnt. For this reason, he returned to England, for better medicine and care. The settlers reported to the tribe that he had died from the explosion and Pocahontas was devastated.

The settlers continued to farm more land, and this made the Powhatan very agitated. This began the First Anglo-Powhatan War, in 1609. Henry Spelman lived among a small group within the Powhatan, called Patawomecks, and they were not always loyal to the larger tribe. The Patawomecks wanted better trading status and an alliance with the English, so they captured Pocahontas, who was visiting their village, by leading her onto Captain Argall's ship and holding her there. Argall requested that the Powhatan release their English prisoners, in return for Pocahontas. The Powhatan returned the people but not the weapons they took in battle.

While in English custody, she stayed in Henricus (land owned by Sir Thomas Dale). This is where she was taught to read and write in English. She was taught through the small amount of books they possessed in the new world, including the family Bible. It was also here that she was introduced to Christianity. In 1614, conflict arose between the settlers and the Powhatans and Pocahontas's father came to settle the argument. She came out and rebuked him, saying "that if her father had loved her, he would not value her less than old swords, pieces, or axes; wherefore she would still dwell with the Englishmen who loved her," speaking of the English family she lived with. Her father relented, for she was no longer in captivity, but came and went freely. With her father's blessing, she also asked to be baptized as a Christian and took the Christian name "Rebecca."

During her time with the English, she met John Rolfe - a wealthy planter in Jamestown, who lost his wife and child on his travels from England, shipwrecked in Bermuda, and then found his way back up to Jamestown. He had just started planting a Bermuda strain of tobacco, and was reaping the wealth from his crops. Pocahontas fell in love and with her father's consent, married John Rolfe. To do this, he also needed permission from the Governor and wrote of the great benefits to the colony if they married. The Governor gave his blessing, as well, and they were married on April 5, 1614. Their son was born in January 1615. This marriage promoted peace between the two people, and they began to trade freely and work together for the common good of the people.

Much like the Spanish, one of the goals of the English was to teach Christianity and convert the indigenous people. Pocahontas was a great example, and few others joined her. To show the Crown that this was possible, they invited Pocahontas and John Rolfe to return to England and be presented to the royal court. This was to show the crown that there was hope of converting the "savage" people (meaning those who were uncivilized, uneducated, and even pagan). June 12, 1616, Pocahontas set out on a very new adventure, with her husband and child, 10 others Christian converts from the Powhatan tribe, and Pocahontas's guardian, the medicine-man Tomocomo, who promised to keep her safe during their travels. Captain John Smith was living in London during the time Pocahontas was in Plymouth. He wrote to Queen Anne about all she had done for him, and asked that she be treated well.

Pocahontas and Tomocomo were entertained at frequent banquets and met so many people, that when they met King James, he was so unattractive and acted like all other guests, that they didn't know who they met, until it was clarified to them after the meeting. She was not a princess, but the London company showed her around as if she were American royalty and presented her father as the greatest ruler of the Powhatan Empire. During her trip she was treated with very high regard and respect and even during Christian Masque, her seat was that of royalty. Her meeting with London's Bishop was reported similarly, "Reverend Patron, the L. Bishop of London, Doctor King, entertained her with festival state and pomp beyond what I have seen in his great hospitality afforded to other ladies."

While in England, she met many influential people, including the Indian who would later be known as Squanto (who would save the Puritans, near Plymouth, in the Americas). But none were more memorable to Pocahontas than when John Smith met with her in England at a social gathering. Remember that she was told that he was dead. At first, she could not meet with him due to her surprise and tears. They met hours later, and he was overjoyed that she spoke English and was so well-educated. According to Smith's record, the Chief knew he wasn't dead, but asked Tomocomo to find him.

In March 1617, Rolfe and Pocahontas boarded a ship for Virginia, but before they hit the ocean, Pocahontas fell severely ill. She was taken ashore and died. No one knows why she died, except that it was a European illness that was not native to the indigenous people. Her last words were "all must die, but tis enough that her child liveth." She is now buried at St. George's Church, Gravesend, England. She will always be known as the woman that brought two nations together. Her strength and love for life would bring peace, and strengthen the respect of the people from which she came.

Activity: Saving from Death and a Reunion — Many people have died too early in the past. Who, in history, would you have liked to have saved from death?

_____

_____

_____

_____

Many have died in the past for a good cause. What good do you think came from this person after they had died? You must come up with one idea.

_____

_____

_____

_____

If you could bring one person back from history, who would you like to meet? Why?

_____

_____

_____

_____

Henry Hudson (1565-1611) (W8:D3)

Henry Hudson was a well-trained seaman, from early in his life, starting as a cabin boy, and making his way up to ship's Captain. The Muscovy Company of England hired him to sail in search for a northern route to Asia. The expedition for a northern route became a race between the French, Dutch, and English, and the winner would control the northern route. The problem was that the ice covered the route for over three fourths (3/4) of the year, so they only had 3 months to search those waters.

1607 Expedition

Hudson took his first shot, sailing with only 10 men and a ship's boy. They reached the East coast of Greenland, and then sailed East to the area later called Hakluyt's Headland, in what is now known as Svalbard, north of the Netherlands. See, at this point they were not sailing to find the northern route over the Americas, but that of Europe and Russia. They wanted to find a way to travel to Asia from any route possible. They found that, because of too much ice, they had traveled too far North and had to turn South, and back to England. He brought back stories of large quantities of whales, which spurred new whaling fleets to travel north to harvest their meat and oil for lamplight.

1608 Expedition

This time, both the British East India and Muscovy Companies joined forces and hired Hudson to sail north of the land now known as Russia. The ice became too thick, though, and he had to return; however, records do show he was able to travel north of the Arctic Circle and make it as far as Novaya Zemlya, near Northern Russia. This is where the ice became too thick to penetrate, and for fear it would crush his ship, they turned around. He turned back near the end of August, still during the summer heat.

1609 Expedition
On this expedition, only the Dutch East India Company would hire Hudson to try again, to sail above modern-day Russia, but by May, he turned around, abandoning this route. Instead, it was still early enough to try a new route. There was a rumor of a northern route above the Americas and Hudson was determined to find it. On his first attempt, he arrived in the New World, near Newfoundland, in early July, and then sailed south to Nova Scotia, Cape Cod, and even as far south as the Hudson River (which he sailed up and claimed for the Netherlands, before returning North up the coast). On this trip, they encountered the First Nations tribes, a group of indigenous tribes that banded together for war against their enemy native nations. Hudson traded with many native tribes on this expedition, trading beaver skins and fur for manufactured goods, like glass and other merchandise, brought for this purpose. When his men ran out of things to trade, their greed got the better of them. According to a journal entry of one of his ship's crew, the men attacked the native village by night, taking the things they could not trade. This was reported in the personal journal of the drunken shipmate, Robert Juet. Remember his name.

Now this entire coastal area of North America had already been discovered and explored by John Cabot's son, Sebastian, in 1508, and Giovanni da Verrazzano, as early as 1524, but it was Hudson who traveled upriver and dedicated the land for the Netherlands - and recorded it by map. By mid-September, they return to Europe after a crew member was killed, by being shot in the neck by a native's arrow. As soon as Hudson arrived, the Ambassador of the Netherlands took his logs and maps and had the land recorded as property of the Netherlands.

1610-1611 Expedition – After his last journey, Hudson was determined to make it to Asia through the Northern route. This time, he had gained the confidence and funding of the London Company and British East India Company, who heard his successes and offered him more funding, supplies, and a new ship, the *Discovery*. He released his contract with the Netherlands and accepted those of his own country. He added to his crew, beyond his normal members: Edward Wilson, as surgeon; Abacuk Pricket, the serving-man of one of the expedition's funders; Thomas Wydowse, a mathematician; and Henry Greene, a good-natured friend. This time, he sailed above Iceland, just south of Greenland. By June, he reached North America in what is now called the Hudson Strait. This proved to them that they had found the Northern Passage and they spent the next few months mapping the area. During this time, Juet stirred up the crew to mutiny, but so loyal were the men to their captain that it fell upon deaf ears and Juet was stripped of his position. Though some called for him to be marooned, the captain had mercy on him, and simply demoted him to the lowest crewmember as they continued their journey. So determined were they to find their passage, that they explored into November, when their ship became stuck in the ice and the crew was forced to head to shore. Staffe, the ship's carpenter, reported it too cold to build shelters; this sent the captain into a rage, and an argument that lasted a few days. Staffe finally agreed to build a single shelter. The men, led this time by Greene, were again stirred up, due to not being supplied more provisions, and became angry with their captain again.

When the ice melted, Hudson wanted to continue his expedition to find the northern passage, but most of his crew was determined to go home. As long as Hudson's navigator, Robert Bylot, was on the Captain's side, the crew knew they could not make it home. It may have been Hudson's transfer of the position of first mate to John King, his illiterate quartermaster, or when he commanded the crew to ration their supplies even more, but Bylot turned and became neutral. The crew was empowered. Led by Juet and Greene, they mutinied in June, leaving Hudson, his teenage son, and seven men, including Staffe - who volunteered to stay with the captain due to his loyalty - adrift in an open rowboat. The marooned tried to keep pace, rowing after the *Discovery,* until the *Discovery* opened their sails to quicken their pace away from the Captain's rowboat. Hudson and crew were never heard from again. On the *Discovery*'s voyage back, the crew turned on each other again, and almost marooned a few other crew members. If not for the fact that they needed Pricket's master to pardon them, they would have thrown him overboard. The *Discovery* returned to England, where the men were arrested. But, because of their knowledge of the New World, they were released, and kept as a source of

information about the conditions and the Northern Route. Many expeditions went to search for Hudson, but never found him. Instead, the area he discovered was named after him and the fur trade by the English, through the Hudson Bay Company, grew quickly, through the information his men brought back.

Activity: Surviving the Northern Passage – If you were stranded in Hudson Bay, thousands of sailing miles away from home, what would you do? This may be your greatest fear, or the greatest adventure you could ever imagine. For this activity, I would like you to come up with a plan, after your men had marooned you on a rowboat. What would you have done to survive or return home? Remember that in your party you have the ship's carpenter, your teenage son, and 6 very ill crewmembers, and it is June 1611. What would you do first, to survive, and next, to be rescued, or escape? Would you interact with natives of the area? What would you do if you were in Hudson's position?

Below is a map to show you how far from England they were and how returning to England was not an option.

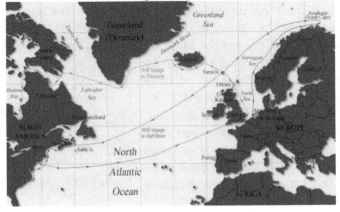

Create a plan in the space below of how you would survive until you could be rescued.

_____

_____

_____

_____

_____

_____

_____

_____

_____

_____

_____

_____

_____

_____

_____

Conquest of Bermuda and the Caribbean (W8:D4)–

Did you know that British colonies still exist? The oldest came by complete accident. It was due to a hurricane that sent a British flag ship, sailing for Jamestown, off course and into the reefs, surrounding uninhabitable islands, to keep it from sinking, with its hundreds of passengers and sailors, and its supplies. The supplies were needed to sustain the people in Jamestown, who were starving. This delay, of nine months, cost the settlers 440 out of 500 lives.

But that was not the Europeans' first contact with the island. The island is recorded to have been found by a Spanish sailor, by the name of Bermúdez. This could easily have been Francisco Bermúdez, who sailed on Columbus's first voyage; Diego Bermúdez, who sailed on Columbus's fourth voyage; or Juan's brother, Diego Bermúdez, who accompanied Ponce de Leon on his 1513 voyage. Yet, there is no record written by Juan Bermúdez of his direct contact with the island, until 1515. The problem was that the sharp rocks and the poor soils kept the Spanish from setting up a settlement on any of the islands. And even though it was on a direct path back to Spain, using a Gulf Stream that passed north of the islands, it was too dangerous to occupy. Examples are those of a French explorer, Russell, shipwrecked in 1570, the English explorer, Henry May, in 1593, and the Spanish sailor, Captain Ramirez, all escaping the islands.

On July 24, 1609, the *Sea Venture*, captained by Sir George Somers, with the London Company, was guided into the reef, so that the hurricane that was brewing behind them would not sink them. This move saved every member on the ship and all their supplies, but destroyed the ship on its way to Jamestown. It took 9 months to build two new ships, the *Deliverance* and the *Patience*, out of wood they found on the islands, and divide the passengers and supplies between the two.

John Rolfe and his wife were aboard the *Sea Venture*, yet he was the only member of his family to make it to Jamestown. He would later fall in love and marry Pocahontas, the Powhatan Chief's daughter, bringing peace between the colony and the native population.

Though a few men stayed in Bermuda after the two ships departed, nothing was recorded of their stay, and it wasn't until a year later before Somers could return to find the men thriving. Now the London Company did not have the patent and permission to colonize Bermuda, so they left the islands alone until 1612, when the Virginia Company was given permission to colonize the island. Sir Richard Moore, the first Governor, returned to the islands to find three men still thriving. The colony was not as successful and was handed back to the Crown. It was later given over to Somers's Company.

Somers subdivided the islands into eight areas, which they called tribes, and allowed 600 settlers, from nine ships, to settle the islands. They began to build forts all around the islands, as their success became well-known. The tobacco, grown in Bermuda, was envied by all other colonies in the area. Exports included sea salt, sugarcane, figs, and pineapples. The people began to establish plantations throughout the islands and in 1616, the island began to import Indian and African slaves to help on these farms. By 1619, Bermuda had over a hundred

African and Native slaves throughout the islands. By 1620, all immigration from Europe had ceased, because there was no more land to sell for new farms. The population had increased so much, that colonists were forced to **emigrate** to other established colonies. The colonists set up their own representative government.

In 1642, the English experienced a civil war in the mainland, which extended out to all its colonies. On the islands, colonists struggled under the control of the King and began to revolt. Puritans and Independents were forced to settle much of the Bahamas, and they were not too happy with the King. In 1649, King Charles was beheaded, and his son Charles II was exiled and replaced by a Commonwealth. In the islands, there was a great division between supporters and dissenters of the Crown, and they took up arms against each other. The new Commonwealth began writing laws that hurt the colonies, including the Prohibitory and Navigation Act, where trade could only be done with English ships. The British Atlantic fleet was sent to enforce the laws, and force allegiance to the Commonwealth.

This was not the only struggle the colony experienced. In 1674, due to four previous slave revolts, a law was put into place that all freed, black indentured servants and slaves must be returned to slavery. In 1682, a new revolt was being planned by a Jamaican slave, named Tom, when two Bermudian slaves turned him in.

Bermuda was a common port for privateers, until Spain and England signed a peace treaty and all privateering was to cease. Those privateers, without many options outside of privateering, turned to piracy. They continued to operate out of Bermuda, mostly from the pirate-claimed island of New Providence. There are fifteen recorded privateers that sailed from this port and attacked the Spanish, using the Gulf Stream just north of the islands to return to Spain. Their crews were a mix of both colonists turned pirates, as well as free and enslaved labor. Bermudian pirates continued to operate, loyal to the crown, until the time of the American Revolution and the War of 1812, where they would assist the British Royal Navy against the Colonists.

Bermuda has a rich history of success and struggles and continues, to this day, as a British colony, struggling for its independence and to be recognized as a sovereign nation. Because of the many benefits of being part of the British Empire, though, they continue to harbor much support for the British connection.

Activity: Bermuda Cooking - Bermuda Johnny Bread
These are simple household ingredients:
¼ cup of sugar (use a ¼ cup)
1 ½ cups of flour (use a 1 cup and ½ cup)
¼ teaspoon of Salt (use a 1/4 tbs)
2 teaspoons of baking powder (use a 1 tbs)
1 egg
½ cup of milk (use a ½ cup)
2 tablespoons of butter (amount found on wrapper)

Directions:
1) Mix flour, sugar, salt, and baking powder. While mixing, slowly add egg and milk, mixing until batter consistency is smooth, and well blended.
2) (Under parental guidance) Melt butter in a frying pan. Spoon a third of the batter into the pan. Fry on low heat until brown. Flip it to toast the other side.
3) Split bread in half, and serve with butter and jam. The island was filled with fruits and sugar, so this was an easy meal to make.

Journal Entry: Settler's Life? – What would life have felt like if you were a settler, coming over from Europe, and finding yourself in a land unknown to you or anyone else? You step foot off the boat and find this new land, beautiful and raw? What would you be feeling? What is the first thing you would do? How would you make this raw land your home? Now, write down your thoughts in your journal. Tell us what life would be like:

Write your Journal Entry Here:

_____

_____

_____

_____

_____

_____

_____

_____

_____

_____

UNIT #9 – MIGRATION - Plymouth and Puritan (W9:D1)

During the **Reformation**, the Church of England broke from the Roman Catholic Church, yet kept many of its practices. The Puritans were a religious group, made up of two groups: the Brownists - the earliest dissenters from the Church of England, and separatist Puritans, who wanted to purify the Church of England (believing it reformed enough). Both groups were forced out of England when they wouldn't agree to the practices of the Church of England, including the government controlling the church (they believed it should instead be a democratic congregation and God). Under English law, it was illegal for anyone not to attend a church controlled by the Church of England, punishable with a fine and then imprisonment. Many underground churches popped up throughout the country, practicing their own beliefs. So England stepped in and began imprisoning these believers. In 1593, a few of their leaders were executed, for sedition against the government. For this, the Puritans decided - together - that they needed to find a place they could settle and live their beliefs free of persecution and control by the government. They first traveled to Amsterdam, in the Netherlands, and petitioned the courts in England for better treatment. The courts and King heard them and accepted one of their requests: to update an English translation of the Bible (the **King James version)**. In Amsterdam, employment was near impossible for them to find, and many ran out of money and had to return to England, and so were driven to make another plan. The King agreed to permit them to settle land in North America, near the Hudson. With the help of the Merchant Adventurer company (which would become the Plymouth Company), they funded their first expedition and set sail for the Americas, aboard the *Mayflower*, in July 1620. The ship that was to accompany them turned around twice, possibly due to sabotage.

Aboard the *Mayflower*, while waiting out the storm, the Puritan men created a pact amongst their leaders and put it to paper. See, while they all wanted to be outside of the King's control, many Puritans wanted to rule their lives with no outside influence, while others wanted to create a rule of governance that would help everyone stay as one. To compromise, they wrote and signed a document that would bring them, as a group, freedom from all outside influences. This would come to be known as the **Mayflower Compact**. This was the governing document for the Plymouth Colony.

> *In the name of God, amen. We, whose names are underwritten, the Loyal Subjects of our dread Sovereign Lord King James, by the Grace of God, of Great Britain, France, and Ireland, King, Defender of the Faith. Having undertaken for the Glory of God, and Advancement of the Christian Faith, and the Honour of our King and Country, a Voyage to plant the first Colony in the northern Parts of Virginia; Do by these Presents, solemnly and mutually, in the Presence of God and one another, covenant and combine ourselves together into a civil Body Politick, for our better Ordering and Preservation, and Furtherance of the Ends aforesaid: And by Virtue hereof do enact, constitute, and frame, such just and equal Laws, Ordinances, Acts,*

Constitutions, and Offices, from time to time, as shall be thought most meet and convenient for the general Good of the Colony; unto which we promise all due Submission and Obedience.

This is what is now considered the first act of freedom against any other sovereign nation in the new world, and the creation of a government for and of the people (though it would take many battles and wars to create an independent nation). Signing the pact was the first law they broke; the second was to disembark to explore Cape Cod Bay, and finally, on December 21, 1620, they left the ship, in the middle of winter. They were short on supplies and, without the ability to farm during the winter, many of them began to starve; half of them died.

Now just a few years before (1614 and 1617), the local indigenous tribe, the Wampanoag people, were hit with a deadly plague - whether from European traders or nature's creation is not certain. What is certain, is that nearly 90-95% of the people died, and much of the land abandoned. The neighboring tribes worried about the plague, so continued to keep their distance. This is where the pilgrims settled, on very fruitful soil. When searching for food, they found a storage of corn and beans leftover, enough to begin the next year's crops.

Back in 1614, English explorers from the Virginia colony came through and captured 27 Indian men, and brought them to Spain to be sold into slavery. A group of Spanish friars intervened, purchased the rest of the slaves and set them free, including a Patuxet-Wampanoag, named Tisquantum (called 'Squanto' by the pilgrims). While with the monks, he was introduced to Christianity and soon converted. He would later become an interpreter on an English expedition sent back to Newfoundland and from there, he left the group to return home in 1619. When he returned, he found that his entire tribe had died.

In the Spring of 1621, those who were strong enough (maybe 6 out of the 100 settlers), began to plant their crops. One day, an Abenaki, by the name of Samoset, came wandering into the village unarmed and spoke to them in English, which he had learned from traders. He warned them that other Indians in the area may be hostile, due to the Spanish taking natives as slaves. This discussion led to further help from other tribesmen, like Squanto, who would interpret for both sides. After all other natives returned home, he stayed to help teach the pilgrims how to farm in this new climate and soil. He also showed the men where the most fertile hunting and fishing waters were. This friendship between the pilgrims and local indigenous tribe opened the door for other tribes to trade with them, including furs and crops. This also led to the Massasoit, or leader of the Wampanoag, forming a peace treaty with the settlers.

When a boy from the colony got lost in the woods and was found by the Nauset tribe, a deal was struck to return him, in exchange for corn to replace the seeds that the pilgrims had unwittingly taken the year before and planted to grow their crops. During these talks, another tribe had kidnapped the Massasoit, Squanto, and a few other Wampanoags, by the Narragansett tribe, and the Puritans sent out a rescue party, led by Myles Standish. When Squanto escaped and the Massasoit was released, the Puritans took the natives that were injured and nursed them back to health. Both acts helped secure good relations with the local tribes.

With this treaty also came a price that the Wampanoag would accept for the pilgrims to purchase land; in return, they would teach the pilgrims how to farm that land. Their harvest was so plentiful in the fall of 1621, that the pilgrims gathered with over 90 tribesmen to celebrate their friendship with prayer, food, and sports. The surviving pilgrims consisted of 4 women, 27 children, and 22 men. Some call this the **First Thanksgiving**, though Virginia had been celebrating them in Jamestown since 1607, with their arrival. Shortly after the celebration, a second ship, the *Fortune*, arrived with 37 new settlers and very little supplies, and the crops did not last the winter, again. The *Fortune* also came with a message from the Merchant Adventurers Company, chastising the settlers for not returning the *Mayflower* with goods to begin repaying the Puritan's debt. They returned the *Fortune* with goods to begin repaying the debt, but it was captured by the French and repayment was not received. In 1623, three more ships arrived with even more settlers, many loyal to the Company, to ensure the repayment of their debts. Upon arrival, many of these settlers decided not to be "enslaved" under the agreement with the company, and settled elsewhere.

In the following years, many ships came with additional settlers, including the *Sparrow*, which brought 60 men who settled Weymouth, Massachusetts. Because of a dispute, started by Myles Standish (again), these settlers, and some tribal leaders, the relationship between colonists and indigenous diminished. The fur trade nearly disappeared, and the open communication disappeared; eventually leading to conflicts, like King Philip's War.

In 1691, the colony, estimated at 3,055 people, merged with the Massachusetts Bay Colony, and created the Province of Massachusetts Bay. To this day, it is still considered the first settlement in New England.

Activity: Thanksgiving (W9:D2) – If you began these lessons in late August or early September, it is probably coming close to the United States' celebration of Thanksgiving. For that, we will be doing some crafts to celebrate a strong harvest and plenty of food.

Part 1: Thanksgiving Celebrations at Home - First, we would like you to list all the steps you would need to take to prepare for Thanksgiving. If you don't have that many traditions, look up other traditions you think would be fun to celebrate:

1. _____

2. _____

3. _____

4. _____

5. _____

6. _____

7. _____

8. _____

9. _____

10. _____

Part 2: Steps to Cook a Turkey – What is Thanksgiving without a turkey? I know, not everyone celebrates Thanksgiving, or celebrates it the same way, but the traditional Thanksgiving - back to the pilgrims - would include a turkey. The next step in this activity is to list all the steps to cook a turkey. Again, you may not cook them, but they did in history; so humor them, by writing down the steps to cook one.

1. _____

2. _____

3. _____

4. _____

5. _____

6. _____

7. _____

8. _____

9. _____

10. _____

11. _____

12. _____

Part 3: Crafting a Turkey – Now there are many ways to craft a turkey. Today you are going to pardon a turkey, meaning they are safe from the carver's knife, and will live to tell the tale. The turkey you will be pardoning is one of your own creation. You can make it out of paper, cardboard, paper plates, or even cookies and candy corn, but try to resist eating that last turkey. Your task is to create a turkey in a craft, and pardon them from the dinner table. Here are a few examples:

King Philip's War (W9:D3) – When Massasoit - the Wampanoag chief - died, his son, Metacom - who went by the English name Philip - replaced his father. Massasoit held a long alliance with the pilgrims, but when Philip took over, he broke this alliance, after many disputes with the colonists, including threatening to take away the tribe's guns after they were used to attack colonists and their native allies. Then, in 1675, three Wampanoags were tried and hung for the murder of a "praying Indian," or native who converted to Christianity. Philip attended the trial and made this his turning point. He sent warriors to attack homesteads throughout Connecticut, Massachusetts, Rhode Island, and Maine. Their tactic was to attack randomly, in different locations, over a six-month span, to keep from being caught. The Colonial Militia was assembled to fight off these attacks, but they were sporadic. Tribes, such as the Narragansetts, tried to stay neutral, but individuals from their tribes would participate, so the colonists couldn't tell who were really on their side. When they caught warriors of these neutral tribes, they would deem those tribes to have broken their treaties.

The militia was made of over 1,000 soldiers and 150 Native allies - the strongest army in the colonies so far. In November 1675, they attacked the Narragansetts, burning their village, and killing around 600. Their leader, Canonchet, retaliated, joining the native coalition.

In the end, the colonist militia won, but not without destroying many towns and native villages. Hundreds died on both sides, economies halted, and relations between colonists and indigenous peoples dissolved. It can be said, the only good that came from the war was that it was fought without any support from any

European government, which began to strengthen the resolve of colonists to separate from outside control.

Activity: Dispute Resolution: Tell of one time when you had to clear up a misunderstanding or a fight with a family member or friend. What happened, that it was needed? Who made you clear it up?

_____

_____

Was it something you wanted to do, or something you were made to do?

_____

_____

How was it resolved?

_____

_____

Did you feel better afterwards?

_____

_____

Journal Entry: Life as a Native American: - We have told you the story of conflicts that took place between the Native Americans and the colonists. Imagine what it would have felt like for you. What would you have experienced if you were a native to the Americas, and foreigners tried to come in and take over your land? What if they simply wanted to live next to you, and not disturb your way of life, how would you feel? Now, write down your thoughts in your journal. Tell us what life would be like:

Write your Journal Entry Here:

_____

_____

_____

_____

_____

_____

_____

_____

_____

_____

UNIT #10: FRENCH - French Exploration (W10:D1)

It was under **Francis I, King of France** that exploration of the New World became essential to their expansion. French fishermen had fished the American east coast for years; Captain Thomas Aubert returned with the first Native ambassador, to share their culture, clothing, transportation, and weapons. Giovanni da Verrazzano may have been among his crew. This intrigued Francis I and he desired to find a shipping route west to Asia.

In 1522, **Ferdinand Magellan's** crew had returned from circumnavigating the globe. This only heightened both science, with the understanding that the world was round, and trade. With Spain in the lead, France was not to be outdone. In 1523, Francis I hired Verrazzano to return to North America and map the entire East Coast, from Spanish owned Florida to Terranova - referred to as "Newfound Land." Their goal was to find a northern route to Asia. Four ships set sail and after devastating weather, only two returned.

After repairing the ships, they set sail along the southern route to Florida, which was under watchful guard of Spain and Portugal. Landing near Cape Fear, in soon-to-be North Carolina, he sent a letter back to King Francis I that this was where the Pacific Ocean was to be reached, but that he would find another way further north, not already discovered by Spain. Traveling North, he discovered the entrance of the Hudson Bay and groups from the **Wampanoag** and **Narragansett**. He continued north around Cape Cod and up to Nova Scotia and Newfoundland, and then returned to France, on July 8, 1524, to express his belief that there was no northern route to Asia. He called the region Francesca, after the

King, but his brother's map named it Nova Gallia (New France).

Verrazzano set out on a second voyage in 1527, to South America, with four ships. Losing one in a storm, he took the other two southward towards Brazil and harvested brazilwood to bring back to France. Verrazzano still could not find a route to the Pacific, so he returned a third time  in 1528, but this is where the story gets murky. Some say his ship was attacked by the Carib cannibals, but some believe him to have turned to piracy, becoming the well-known **Jean Fleury**. No one knows. Unlike Magellan and Cortes, Verrazzano did not have a publicist, or anyone to further his legacy.

Activity: Trust Experiment – This is a family/classroom activity: everyone gets to participate. Create a maze, in a room, with obstacles on the ground (make sure you can get through them) that you will have to guide someone blindfolded through. They will do the same for you. First, give them as much time to go through it as possible, then make them do it in a shorter, set amount of time.

How did doing it blindfolded make you feel?

_____

How did you do with someone else's help?

_____

Jacques Cartier (1491-1557) (W10:D2) –

Born into wealth, James Cartier became a highly respected mariner for the Duchy of Brittany, a medieval feudal state established on a peninsula on the West coast of France. When the two governments (France and Brittany) united, Cartier was introduced to King Francis I directly by Bishop Jean Le Veneur. The king was in search of a navigator to hire, to map out the entire east coast of the New World, find gold and treasures, and find a route to Asia. Le Veneur presented Cartier to the King, because Cartier already had experience sailing to Newfoundland and Brazil.

On April 20, 1534, Cartier set sail. He arrived 21 days later, much different than Columbus and all those who traveled closer to the equator! While there, he mapped the Gulf of St. Lawrence and met with two indigenous tribes, including a brief visit with the Mi'kmaq tribe, (whom he traded with), and then the St. Lawrence Iroquoians. Cartier's men had been working to plant a cross, to lay claim to the area for France, when the natives came upon them. Understanding what the Frenchmen were doing, the mood soured. Though there is some disagreement by historians on what happened, during a possible struggle, two of the Chief's sons were captured. After negotiations, the Chief agreed that the sons should travel with Cartier back to France, on the condition that they bring back European goods that they could trade. Note: During this voyage, they hunted hundreds of seabirds related to penguins. Cartier returned to France, in September 1534.

Since Cartier had made an oath with the Iroquoian Chieftain to return his sons with tradeable goods, he made arrangements to return the next year. They sailed with three ships this time, directly into the Gulf of Lawrence and up the St. Lawrence River, to the tribe's capital, Stadacona, and then Hochelaga, where they met up with Chief Donnacona. Cartier was convinced that the river was the Northern Passage to the Pacific, but he was halted by rapids and could not go any further. He only spent a few days with the Iroquoian tribe, before realizing they had to stay the winter. Being provided land by the tribe, they created a fort to hold them over through the winter, and began to prepare supplies to keep them alive through the brutal winter to come. It was so bad, that the river froze over about 2 meters thick in ice, encased in four feet of snow. Besides the weather, scurvy set in among the tribe, first, and then spread to the Frenchmen, leaving around 50 Iroquoians dead. It was the tribe that saved the French, by telling them of a drink (later called Spruce beer) that was used to cure scurvy. 85 out of Cartier's 110-member crew survived. He declared it a miracle, and the tribe Godsends.

On his return, Cartier invited Donnacona to travel back to France and share the tales of the New World - including the Kingdom of Saguenay, which was to be full of gold and other treasures. He also brought back many treasures of the New World. Arriving in France on July 15, 1536, he returned to a hero's welcome, especially by the King, who accepted much of this treasure and the stories from Donnacona. Francis I quickly ordered Cartier back to the New World, to colonize the area and rule it as "Captain General." Yet it took them 'til 1541 to return. During that time, though they were all treated well, the visiting Iroquoians and Chief Donnacona died. So, in 1541, they were to return with the sole purpose of finding the Kingdom of Saguenay and its many treasures, as told by the Chief. Though he promised Cartier command, Francis I named his close friend Jean-Francois de La Rocque de Roberval Lieutenant General of New France. Roberval sent Cartier in an advanced party of five ships, back to Canada.

Cartier had finally arrived early enough to plant a crop and secure a settlement and two forts, naming the settlement Charlesbourg-Royal. The men began collecting what they thought were diamonds and gold, only to later find them to be simple quartz and iron pyrites (fool's gold). After unloading the cattle, supplies, and settlers, two of the ships returned to France for more supplies and settlers. Cartier set off in search of Saguenay, but was turned around, due to harsh weather. When he returned, he found that the tribe had turned against them. The French were attacked, and 35 settlers were killed before securing the fort. After another brutal winter, Cartier decided to return to France. He met up with Roberval on his way home and, though he wanted Cartier to return with him, Cartier escaped and returned to France - many think with a hull full of gold and diamonds.

Roberval, on the other hand, took this opportunity to maroon his niece, Marguerite, and her lover, on the "Isle of Demons," offshore of Quebec, to claim her riches when she was reported dead and pay off his many debts.

She, and her lover, survived. While marooned, she gave birth, and the family was rescued and returned to France. She became a celebrity after tales of her rescue, yet no actions were taken against Roberval.

Activity: Cooperative Digital Escape Room – Cartier and Roberval's niece were both stuck in hard situations, but were able to escape. This activity is part of an escape room, where your family, classmates, or friends are trying to discover a way into a lockbox for a prize. You will be setting up this escape room, but you can get help to plan it. Below are the steps you need to take. PLEASE don't lock them in a room and make them try to get out - leave that to the professional designers!

Step #1 – Find a lockbox or small safe with a number code on the exterior. You are going to give them riddles and clues around the room to solve, to find each number - and what order they go in. Make the content of the lockbox something they really want or desire, including food, toys, money (if you have to), or prizes. Any local hardware or general store will have it, or you can make your own out of a box around your house and they have to guess the code. If you are looking for a pre-made kit, try: teacheveryday.com/escape-room-in-the-classroom/

Step #2 – Get organized, by finding five riddles or clues you can make that will lead them to one of the numbers. If possible, make the clue part of the room, so you don't have to change the room around. Examples would be to find how many clocks there are in the room or find a hidden number. Be creative, but don't make it too hard. Find a way to direct people to that clue. Then, the fifth clue should be how to organize the numbers. You could also make them coincide with history, math, or science.

3. Tell a story – with every escape room there should be a backstory. Help the players feel like part of the game.

4. Release the hounds - as in, let's play your game. These are a lot of fun and you will learn something new each time you hold one of these. Write down your experiences and clues so you can use them again. Don't overthink it and if your players need help, don't hesitate to give them verbal hints on how to find and answer your clues. And most important - have fun!

Part 2 – Write down the trivia/clues you created for future use. You may have found some really good ones that you don't want to forget in the future.

1. _____

_____

_____

2. _____

_____

_____

3. _____

_____

4. _____

_____

5. _____

_____

_____

6. _____

_____

_____

7. _____

_____

_____

8. _____

_____

_____

9. _____

_____

New France (W10:D3)– Since Giovanni da Verrazzano's first trip to the east coast of North America, to the first French settlement at Charlesbourg-Royal, this northern territory was considered "claimed" by France, and would make up much of what would be known as Quebec, Prince Edward Island, and Nova Scotia. French claimed land, though, would extend all the way down to Mexico. To claim this land, much more was needed. x

Since its first French travelers, who were simple fishermen sailing the Atlantic, there has always been a market for crops and merchandise coming from the New World. Gold was not the only commodity for which Europeans were looking. Some of the greatest materials to be brought back to France consisted of wood, native crafts, crops, and - the most desired from the Northern Territories - fur. Remember that the wildlife in France and England were nearly hunted and harvested to extinction. The wildlife was seen as more of a commodity than nature to be admired. Because of the lack of supply for furs and pelts, French trading companies, and their trappers, found their way south from their first landing. Here, they would hunt animals of all types, thought to be an endless supply in this undiscovered land of the Americas. These groups, entirely made up of men, would travel wherever they found animals to hunt, bringing back only their pelts, to sell to France.

The indigenous people would also trade the French furs and other commodities for manufactured items, such as glass beads; the only thing the Europeans would not trade was iron made weapons. Weapons were not traded for many reasons. Remember that, at that time, every gun and sword was made by hand and were awfully expensive, so it wasn't only that the Europeans didn't want the natives to have guns for a possible uprising, but also that they couldn't afford to lose them.

Much like the English, there were Protestant settlers that were forced to leave France to be able to live out their faith in peace. Their other choice was to convert to Catholicism. Under threat of execution, one million converted, and 500,000 fled France. They found their way to almost any settlement that would take them, including Brazil, where they built forts to protect them from the Portuguese; South Africa, where they were designated land by the Dutch; and North America. One of these groups were the Huguenots, Protestants who held to the reforms on faith made by **John Calvin**. They would come to settle in English and Spanish claimed areas, such as Fort

Carolina in Spanish-owned Florida. They tried to take this land and establish a fort of their own, but it was soon attacked and taken over by Spanish Admiral, Pedro Menéndez de Avilés, who then turned it into **St. Augustine**. Those protestants that were captured were executed. Remember, because they wouldn't convert, they were not allowed to settle in New France. They then turned to the Dutch again, and settled in the Dutch colony of New Netherland. They found peace in the British colony of Nova Scotia and the lands around Hudson Bay.

While the Dutch and British were building settlements throughout North America, the French were working to establish their own. French trading posts began to pop up throughout the land, starting with Sable Island, off the coast of Acadia, in 1598, and many more over the span of only a few years. Some French settlers tried to establish Port Royal again, but it was destroyed in 1613; the settlers who survived scattered and started multiple settlements throughout the area.

In 1608, King Henry IV sponsored **Samuel de Champlain**, Pieere Dugua, and Sieur de Mons to settle what was to be the first sustainable colony in New France, Quebec city. He sent 28 men to settle the land, but many died. More and more settlers would travel there only to die from the harsh weather. By 1630, though hundreds had come, only 103 survived. From the start, Champlain had a shrewd idea: he would align himself with three larger tribes in the area - the Algonquin, the Huron, and Montagnais - and fight with them, against their enemies - the Iroquois. By this time, the Iroquois and the French were already sworn enemies of each other. In 1609,

Champlain, two French soldiers, and the allied tribes attacked. With this win against the Iroquois, these tribes solidified a relationship with the French, and would allow them to stay and trap where needed. This would reassure the establishment of this territory called New France. Champlain's relationship with the indigenous people also allowed him to send young Frenchmen to live among their tribes, learning their language and cultures. They would then learn what the French needed to survive in their harsh wilderness.

With the Iroquois packing up and moving south after their great defeat, the French began to move south in settling this territory. The French and Iroquois would continue this war as they expanded their territory.

The English and French were also competing, not only in Europe, but in the colonies. While the English colonies were thriving, the French were struggling. To boost France's presence, Louis XIII gathered the *Company of One Hundred Associates* to invest in New France, and with promises of riches, made them fund the strengthening of New France. Champlain was made Governor over the territory. The most prominent rule was that the settlers had to be Catholic; Protestants were required to renounce their faith or move to the English colonies. The French also sent missionaries to convert the native population within their territory, sending over Jesuit priests to live among them and work to convert. In the colonies, the people lived under a near feudal system of farming, with landowners dividing their land among the common folk, and allowing them to rent the land for a portion of their crop.

In 1627, the city of Quebec was ransacked by three English privateers. With only 85 settlers, there wasn't much they could do to stop them. In 1629, the French expanded into the St. Lawrence River Valley, which upset the British, who then attacked and seized Quebec City, until 1632, when they relinquished it. During that time, they continued to establish smaller colonies. After the death of Champlain the Bishop of Quebec took power.

During the 1600s, many Jesuit priests traveled to New France to explore the new world and do missionary work among the Indigenous people, including **Charles Albanel**. Much like Mother T
eresa, of recent times, Albanel served the people - both settlers and indigenous, alike - during two outbreaks, including the smallpox epidemic of 1688. During this time, he became ill, from contact with those that were infected, but he continued to serve as much as possible. Afterwards, he became a cultural expert and interpreter between the French and Indian population.

In 1663, New France was taken back from the *Company of One Hundred Associates* by Louis XIV, and the French government began paying settlers to move to the New World, to stimulate their expansion. The colonies grew from a few hundred, to a few thousand, and the French continued to expand south and west, all the way down the Mississippi to Louisiana and Texas. The settlement of Villa-Maria, now called Montreal Island, became the

French center for fur trade and fisheries in the Atlantic. In 1627, the Company of New France was permitted to hunt, trap, and trade furs and pelts throughout French territories. This would be an economic boom to New France, increasing taxes for the city, as well as the country of France. The high taxation caused many trappers to rebel, and begin selling on the black market.

Activity: Establishing your first Fort – In the 17th and 18th centuries, companies from France, England, and the Netherlands would travel to territories claimed by their countries, gather natural materials, and bring them to their country, or other countries, to sell. If you were to start a company in New France and could gather and sell any commodity, what would it be? Ask these questions:

1. What would you sell? (Examples: wood, fur, crafts)

_____

2. Would you process it, or sell it raw to your country?

_____

Other Questions to Ask Yourself:

3. Would you limit how much you would gather or gather as much as possible, as fast as possible?
4. Would you allow others in your market and, if so, would you try to regulate how much they sell?
5. Would you report back to the crown how much you earned, or lie and possibly be sentenced to be executed?
7. Would you enter your neighboring country's land to collect this commodity? Would it be worth it?

Journal Entry: Loyalist? – Which country would you like to have explored for? Which do you think would have treated you the best, and allowed you to settle the land as you saw fit? Here are the countries to choose from: Spain, British, France, Netherlands, Italy, or Portugal. Give an explanation of your answer, and why you think you would have liked to have sailed for them. Now write down your thoughts in your journal. Tell us what life would be like.

Write your Journal Entry Here:

_____

_____

_____

_____

_____

_____

_____

_____

_____

_____

UNIT #11: JOINING COLONIES - 13 Colonies (W11:D1)

 As you may have guessed, the 13 colonies all started at different times, to later become the states of the United States. They also didn't start off as the 13 British colonies, for they were all owned by different countries, including Spain, France, England, Dutch, and Puritans.

As James I, King of England, took power of England, and joined England, Scotland, Ireland, and Wales, to become Great Britain, he, like his predecessor Queen Elizabeth, and all his successor's afterwards, desired to expand their control by discovering new land in the New World.

In 1606, James I gave patents to both the Plymouth Company and London Company to establish settlements in the Americas. The London Company established the Colony and Dominion of Virginia, starting with the establishment of Jamestown. When the Puritans left for the New World and found Plymouth, they tried to leave the crown behind, but were unsuccessful, due to the debt they owed the Plymouth Company for their travel expenses. The company also established other colonies; some that were short lived, and those, like Plymouth, that would become successful.

The Dutch, Swedish, and French established settlements in North America, but most succumbed to the British just before the final colony, Georgia, was established in 1732, to finalize the British control over the east coast of North America. From 1660 to the end of the American Revolution, the British controlled the colonies through a single department, called the Southern Department, and a single committee, called the Board of Trade and Plantations.

Here are the 13 colonies and who established them:

Massachusetts (British charter-1691)	Puritans (GB)
New Hampshire (1629)	John Wheelwright (GB)
Connecticut (1662)	Thomas Hooker (GB)
Rhode Island (1663)	Roger Williams (GB)
Delaware (1664)	Peter Minuit (Swedish)
New York (1686)	Duke of York (Dutch)
New Jersey (1702)	Lord Berkeley (Netherlands)
Pennsylvania (1681)	William Penn (GB)
Virginia (1624)	London Company (GB)
Maryland (1632)	Lord Baltimore (GB)
North Carolina (1729)	Virginians (GB)
South Carolina (1729)	Royal Charter of Charles II (GB)
Georgia (1732)	James Oglethorpe (GB)

*GB = Great Britain

Everything south was owned by Spain...

Activity: Can you name all the Thirteen Colonies?

1.
2.
3.
4.
5.
6.
7.
8.
9.

Finding of New York Colony (1624) (W11:D2)
The colony of New York was inhabited by two competing tribes of indigenous people: **the Iroquois** and **the Algonquin**. These two opposing tribes were divided into smaller groups, known as nations, which would normally have their own language. The Iroquois was a confederacy of 5 tribal nations, self-named Haudenosaunee ("People of the Longhouse"). Now, a confederacy of nations was an agreement between tribes, to work, trade, and fight together against other nations that may attack one, or a few, of the collective tribes. The Iroquois Confederacy was made up of these main tribes: Mohawk ("People of the Flint"); Oneida ("People of Standing Stone"); Onondaga ("People of the Hills"); Cayuga ("People of the Great Swamp"); and Seneca ("Great Hill People"). Though they were mostly peaceful among each other, if a common enemy came against one of them, the nations would respond together. Their nations lived more inland, to the west, and made up mostly around the Great Lakes area - both in the United States and Canada. Their enemies to the east were the Algonquin people.

The Algonquin language was made up of 17 different dialects of the common language, spoken by 24 nation tribes who lived closer to the coast, stretching up the northern east coast of North America. They, like the Iroquois, had an oral agreement between their nations, but contention would stir up, at times, and they would settle it amongst themselves. They would also ban together, though, to take on their enemy - the Iroquois.

These two groups were always fighting and taking each other as slaves, and stealing from one another. In early American native culture, when a tribe came in and attacked your village, the automatic response, after the battle, was not to seek revenge, but instead, to pick up and move. This is why their boundaries were very fluid and changed constantly, though they were not always fighting each other. Most of the time, they would spend their days harvesting very distinct crops, including hunting and fishing. Their cultures were specific to each nation. This allowed each to govern their families and livelihood as they saw fit, generally having a Chief over a tribe (who would govern their own distinct group, with many of these groups in each nation). So, when the Europeans showed up, there were different responses to the new visitors: both contentious and cooperative.

Now, even though John Cabot's son, Sebastian, was the first European to sail and explore this area in 1508 - under contract from the English - and Giovanni Verrazzano explored it for the French, in 1524, it was Henry Hudson, years later (in 1609) to float the ship Halve Maen (Half Moon) up the Hudson River, exploring more of this area, and claiming it for the Netherlands. Though he was English, he was, at that point, employed by the **Dutch East India Company**. When Hudson returned to England, the Dutch Ambassador took possession of his sailing logs, though the English were not happy with it and demanded the paperwork. They wanted to claim the land, but Sebastian and Verrazzano simply explored the coast, never claiming it for England or France. In 1611-1612, the Admiralty of Amsterdam sent two expeditions to survey and map the land, distinguishing that land officially for the Dutch. Then, they sent their first fur trading mission, led by Adriaen Block - with the help of **Juan Rodriguez** (son of an African mother and Portuguese sailor), who was to serve as a translator between the natives and the Dutch. Block set out to trap in this new world, but when a dispute formed between him and a few other traders about their boundaries, Rodriguez broke away to live on his own among the people on Manhattan Island. The natives very much liked trading for his ironware, and they came from throughout the Algonquin lands to trade. The traders returned to the Netherlands, while Rodriguez continued to trade, being considered the first merchant the indigenous people trusted. When more traders arrived, Rodriguez became their middleman, with the Natives.

The fur traders returned to the Netherlands to report about the conditions, which sparked great interest. In 1614, the Dutch began sending expeditions to explore this land, establishing fur trading posts further inland, near current day Albany, called Fort Nassau. The Dutch companies were very competitive with each other, and wanted the most land and return on their investment, as quickly as possible. This competition led to the Dutch government's Republic of the Seven United Netherlands to create regulations within the new colony. Many of these companies created an alliance and, with Block's map, pushed the government to give them the sole patent for the area, but was only a three years contract.

The **Dutch West India Company**, who was given patents for West Africa, decided that they wanted to expand their mission and lead expeditions to settle parts of the New World. In 1620, they appealed to the Seven United Netherlands for a patent to set up smaller settlements throughout North America, which would have a military presence, to expand the fur trade along the east coast. The assembly agreed and began small posts throughout the northern east coast. Colonization began to pick up, with the Dutch being forced out of Brazil by the Portuguese. The Portuguese took the rich sugar plantations of South America and moved in to colonize most of Brazil (which is why Brazilians speak Portuguese, instead of Dutch, English, or Spanish).

The Mohawk tribe controlled a near monopoly on trading with the Dutch, because their territory span included most of current-day New York, from Albany to the coast. Now, for every settlement that was established, a Dutch law was made that it had to be purchased from the tribe that occupied the land or that controlled the territory. It could not be taken, or claimed. Something of high value needed to be traded for them to buy the land. The Dutch would trade manufactured goods for land, fur, and other merchandise they wanted from the tribes. The conflict came because Europeans and Algonquin saw ownership of land very differently. The settlers believed that ownership meant that they had full rights to fish, farm, hunt, and settle the lands for which they traded. The natives would simply pick up and travel, as they were nomadic people, but would return seasonally, even living among the Dutch settlers. The natives did not intend to give up access to the land and the settlers disputed where they could operate and settle the purchased land. This miscommunication would lead to conflict, and even violence in some areas; in other areas, they lived as a multicultural society.

The name New Netherlanders was given to those living in the colony, but it was not only made up of those from the Netherlands, or Dutch, but of English, French, German, Africans, Indians, and natives who lived among them. This was truly a multicultural society, with Dutch as the common language. That's right - the tribes learned their language, and the Dutch learn their tribal dialects.

Now the relationships with the native population were essential for Dutch fur trades, and they worked with both the Algonquin and the Iroquois to trade and gain access to those hunting grounds, trading manufactured goods to gain access to their land. The Dutch were not the only nation to be working with the Iroquois on these trade routes, though. The French were coming in from the north and securing cooperation with the natives, as well. The European companies, who ran the fur trade, were just as competitive as the tribes, leading to conflicts, allegiances, and lucrative arrangements.

In 1624, New Netherland was established as a province of colonized settlements throughout the New York area, from British-claimed Cape Code, south, to the Delaware area. By doing this, their land came close to the English, and this began to stir up tension. Two years later, they moved the capital to the secure island of Manhattan, buying the land from the local native tribes, the Lenape and Wappinger, making certain the arrangement was clear. There, they built a settlement, near the southern tip, called New Amsterdam. To entice new settlers, they promised large plots of land, rights, and privileges for anyone who would travel to the New World.

Years before the area was colonized, the Dutch Republic signed into law the *Union of Utrecht*, which gave everyone freedom of religion, that "everyone shall remain free in religion and that no one may be persecuted or investigated because of religion." The

Dutch West India Company. though, started an "official" church in the New World, called the Reformed Church. and made it the official institution of the colonies.

There were many free black colonial members living among the settlers, but in 1625, the West India Company imported 11 African slaves. As was law at that time, they were given rights, such as testifying in court, signing legal documents, civil actions against whites in courts, and were permitted to live as family units. They were employed by the settlers to work as farmers, fur traders, and builders, and lived among the settlers, being married, and baptized in the same Dutch church. They were even given a set amount of time they could work for a single person, and they were allowed to work extra hours, for pay, from their employers or other settlers.

Remember how the relationship with the indigenous people was very fragile? Well, when Willem Kieft became Director of New Netherland, in 1638, his first conflict was with the Tappan and Weckquaesgeek tribes, who were pushed out of their land by the English settlers, and so moved to Dutch territories. Kieft demanded tributes from the two tribes, which was ignored. When a settler was killed and the perpetrator hid amongst the tribes, Kieft decided to punish them, by ransacking their village; but like many politicians, he organized a committee called the Council of Twelve Men, and made them do his dirty work. They denied his request to punish the tribes and instead, this council began to gather grievances against the Dutch Company. Kieft quickly dismissed them, and attacked the two tribes, killing about 130 men, women, and children. This set off other local tribes and they began raids throughout the settlements, forcing the survivors to gather in Fort Amsterdam. For the next two years, the tribes raided and plundered the province, until finally, the Chief of the tribes and Kieft called for a truce. It was due to his actions that the settlers wrote to the States General of the Netherlands condemning Kieft, and the entire West India Company, for mismanagement, and demanded freedom and full rights in the territory.

Just before 1647, the fur trade was deregulated, and land ownership was given to the "New Netherlanders," instead of the Company. The people became very entrepreneurial and began trading with each other and the Dutch Company, but as individuals, instead of entities controlled by the Company or government. By the time the new director arrived, they were experiencing exponential growth. There was also great conflict among the New Netherlanders, the Dutch government, and the West India Company. The English were beginning to encroach on Dutch land from the north, and the Swedes from the south. Because of all this turmoil, the Dutch began to limit the powers of the West India Company and began giving the locals governance to themselves. In 1652, the Director was recalled. At the same time, the first Anglo-Dutch War broke out.

In March of 1664, Charles II, King of England, Scotland, and now Ireland, demanded they take New Netherlands for church and state. He sent a fleet of frigates into New Amsterdam's harbor and demanded their surrender. They met no resistance, and were able to walk in and capture the city. The locals did not struggle. While they had been asking for years for the Dutch to defend the colony, they were too busy with the Anglo-Dutch War that was taking place. The English renamed it New York.

In the Articles of Surrender, the colonists were able to secure principles of religious tolerance; at the same time, many white Dutch men were taken as prisoners of war, and sold into slavery. The English also destroyed Mennonite villages and other settlements of those who would not accept English rule. In 1673, the Dutch retook New Netherlands with a fleet of 21 ships. In 1674, during the Third Anglo-Dutch war, the Dutch became bankrupt, fighting the English and French in two different wars. New Netherland ceded to English rule, once again.

Activity: Dutch Indulgence - Time to make cookies:
Ingredients
1 cup unsalted butter
1 egg - room temperature
1 cup sugar
2 tsp vanilla extract
2 1/2 cups flour
1 tsp baking powder
1/4 tsp salt

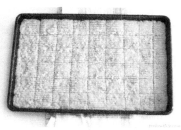

Instructions:
    1. Before you begin, preheat the oven to 300°.
    2. Mix the softened butter and sugar together in a small bowl. After liquifying, beat in the egg and vanilla.
    3. Mix the flour, salt, and baking powder in a bowl.
    4. Mix dry and wet ingredients. It will turn crumbly.
    5. Pat down ingredients evenly into an 11x14 pan.
    6. For decoration, draw lines or designs with a fork.
    7. Bake for 30 minutes and they turn light golden.
    8. Cut it into squares while still warm and let it cool.
    9. Most importantly, enjoy your dessert.

Anglo-Dutch Wars (1652- 1784) (W11:D3)

The Dutch, English, French, Spanish, and Portuguese were all very competitive to claim parts of the New World and explore its fertile lands. Many wars broke out across the waters; ships were pillaged, stolen, or sunk. Spanish ships were constantly being attacked or stolen by all their competitors, but when it came to taking over the fertile soils of North America, no war was as significant as the Anglo (meaning English) – Dutch Wars. Exploration was not the only reason for these groups to battle; the religious dominance over the New World was also a great driving factor for those fighting in the war. The fight was between the Roman Catholic Church, and the newer claimed moderate faith of Protestants.

In the early 1600s, the Dutch fought with the Catholic Habsburg Dynasty of Austria, in the Eight Year War, while exploring the New World in areas such as modern-day New York and Delaware. The Dutch East India Company found much success in India and Indonesia, trading on the spice trade routes, and Dutch privateers had made many successful captures of Spanish ships.

By the early 1700s, the Portuguese made a truce and began to trade heavily with the Dutch. The Dutch merchant fleet was growing to become the largest in all of Europe. The Spanish signed the Peace of Münster treaty, in 1648, and their war came to an end. The Dutch began to decommission their military, which led to a Civil War amongst the Dutch - especially those in the New World, as they felt they were being poorly protected, and demanded more support. No other colony was more vocal about this than the New York colony.

The English, on the other hand, in the 16th century, built up the greatest naval military to conduct privateering against Spanish treasure ships, which only funded more military and privateers. This was known as the Anglo-Spanish War. Protestant King, James I, wanted peace with Spain and the Catholics, so he signed a treaty with Spain and outlawed privateering for a time, and then neglected his Royal Navy. Charles I, while sympathizing with the Catholics and Spain, reconstructed his Navy. During this time, Charles made secret agreements with Spain to fight the Dutch sea power.

During the English Civil War of 1642, the Navy was again neglected, and weakened because of divisions in the war. King Charles was beheaded, and his predecessor, **Oliver Cromwell,** succeeded in bringing the country back together. He then revamped the Navy to focus on one great task: to cripple the Dutch merchant and naval fleets. He turned the country's anger towards the Dutch as their common enemy. Their grievances stemmed from fishing in English waters, to the Dutch forcing England out of India and Indonesia, to the Dutch's free trade attitude (which circumvented the English's high tax and control structure). The Spanish forces were also up for grabs, because the Spanish Empire was beginning to crumble at the end of the Thirty-Year War in 1648.

Cromwell feared the political strength of Orange, a region of France, and the Colonists of the Republic in the New World, who both supported Charles I when the King was beheaded. To gain support, he joined forces with the Dutch in taking the fallen Spanish colonies, a very lucrative endeavor. This treaty was one sided, with the English as benefactor, and the Dutch saw through the deception, which led to war.

First War (1652–1654) – As the Dutch began to decommission much of their Navy, because of their treaty with Spain, the English began to purchase and recommission them, growing their Navy force. Instead, the Dutch grew their merchant fleet and continued to trade throughout the world, yet, due to their treaty with Spain, were not allowed to trade with most of Southern Europe. The English, in 1651, signed the Navigation Acts, only allowing English ships to trade in England, which shrunk the reach of the Dutch traders and made it lawful for English privateers to attack Dutch ships.

With the increase in hostility, the Dutch felt they had to respond. They began to support armed merchant ships. The English demanded that other ships lower their flags, in respect for England, when two ships passed; the Dutch refused, leading to the first conflict on the sea (the Battle of Dover), which led to England declaring war on the Dutch, on July 10, 1652. Though battles occurred all the time at sea, the first major conflict was the Battle of the Kentish Knock, with the Dutch sailing 62 ships and 1900 cannons, compared to the English's 68 ships and 2,400 cannons. The Dutch were forced to withdraw, not due to the lack of guns, but the internal struggle between the ships, which nearly ended the first war.

The Dutch succeeded in driving away the English ships in the smaller Battle of Leghorn, near Italy, where they gained most of the control over the Mediterranean. The English had also lost control of the English Channel. The final battle occurred on August 10, 1653, at the Battle of Scheveningen, which finally exhausted the two fleets to sign the Treaty of Westminster, on April 5, 1654. Afterwards, England went to war with Spain.

The Second War (1665-1667) – Peace did not last long. The English merchant companies, like the Levant Company and East India Company, saw the success of their businesses during this time of turmoil with the Dutch, and they began pressuring England to restart the war. They suggested making every ship available and filling them with a crew that would be paid by the plunders of the Dutch ships they attacked. Before the war had even begun, the English ships sailed across the Atlantic, straight into the harbor of New Amsterdam, to find it defenseless. In 1665, the English fleet set sail and captured and plundered dozens of Dutch ships, which were then sunk, or released crippled. The Dutch trading industry suffered greatly; then the Dutch fought back.

The Dutch quickly learned the strategy the trading companies had learned: they were more profitable during times of war. By 1666, Dutch trade recovered and began to thrive, taking trade away from the English. The English did get their revenge, setting fire to destroy a fleet of 140 Dutch ships and subsequently, the city of West-Terschelling, Netherlands. The Dutch sought revenge for that, and so started the **Great Fire of London.**

Something else happened during this time that hurt England greatly: the people began to suffer from the plague. Their cities were ravished by this disease, and so were their ships. This nearly crippled the English efforts. In 1667, the Dutch laid another blow on the English, as they attacked the English fleet, harbored for the night, near Upnor Castle. During this attack, they plundered many ships, captured the town Sheerness, and stole the HMS Royal Charles - flagship of the English. This was the worst defeat that the Royal Navy would ever experience. This crippled the English war efforts and ended the Second war. One last battle was launched by the Dutch, when they sailed from New Amsterdam to Virginia, destroyed a British ship in the harbor, and attacked and plundered the Hampton Roads fort. The news sent London into a panic, as the people began to revolt against Charles II. He quickly sent Ambassadors to sign a peace treaty with the Dutch.

Even though they won, and could demand reparations (rewards back from the English), they did not ask for New Amsterdam back, but only the sugar plantations down the east coast of the Americas. New Netherland stayed under English law, when the Treaty of Breda was signed.

Third War (1672-1674) (W11:D3) – You think this would have taught the two countries a lesson on attacking each other, but in 1672, as soon as the English fleet was rebuilt, they were at it again (though they did not have the support of the English people). It was the secret treaty with the French that pushed them to assist Louis XIV in his attacks on the Dutch, during the Franco-Dutch War. The French and English forces were prevented from attacks, and after many failed attempts, the people rose up to demand Charles make peace once again.

During this time, the Dutch briefly took back New York. They installed the first ever Dutch Governor, as all others had been appointed by the Dutch East India Company. It was now named New Orange, after the Dutch Royal House of Orange. Though the Dutch had won the war, they relinquished the colony to the British, in exchange for the plantation colony of Surinam, which was more profitable. It's still a country in South America today.

Fourth and Final War (1780-1784) – The English had learned their lesson; their people's voices were heard, and peace was kept for over 100 years. This was partially due to the Dutch attacking England in 1688, during the *Glorious Revolution,* where the Dutch crossed the channel and dethroned James II, who was replaced by his Protestant daughter Mary and her Dutch husband, William of Orange. Orange was a region of France. He joined the fleets of England and Dutch to combat the French. The King gave the Royal Navy much respect, and privileges to earn their loyalty, and keep it. By 1707, Scotland formally united with England, to create the Kingdom of Great Britain. The fleet became the most dominant military force in all the world. The Dutch freely traded in England and the economy of both kingdoms flourished. The defeat in the Americas during the American Revolution, and the support of the colonists over the British, created a resentment that led to the fourth and final war. The Dutch Navy was a fraction of what it once was; the British Navy was diminished because of the war in the Americas. So, this was not as much a war as the two countries rebuilding their fleet, in order to attack (though not much occurred until the French Revolution and the Napoleonic Wars, in 1793-1815, when the French basically left their presence in the Netherlands, annexing the country, in 1810). The Dutch and English had small battles and scuffles in the future, but nothing like the first three wars, that had sent hundreds of ships to the deep dark burial grounds in the sea. Peace was built from the mutual respect they had for the two European countries, and not through the battles themselves.

Activity: The Art of Propulsion – The ships of the past are nothing like what we have today. Back then, the ships were propelled forward by the wind in their sails; now, they move using large propellers under the ship. Today, we are going to experiment with the difference between wind power and propulsion. Check out this activity at: http://www.huntthepast.com/propellervswind/ https://www.youtube.com/watch?v=F8-84J8vtUg

First: Draw your ship. What would your ship look like?

Next, do the activity, and then come back to these questions afterwards:

1. What difference do you see between using a propeller and using a sail?

_____

_____

_____

2. What are the similarities between the two?

_____

_____

3. What is the advantage of using wind?

_____

_____

_____

4. What is the advantage of using a propeller?

_____

_____

Journal Entry: Colonial Life: - We have now told you the story of what it was like to be in a new colony or settlement - basically the frontier of North America. Now, tell us what it would have felt like to have lived in colonial America. What would you have felt, and thought. Would you have feared attack by the local tribes, been anxious about disease and hunger, excited for new experiences, entrepreneurial for all the opportunities, or a mix of all? Write down your thoughts in your journal. Tell us what it would be like and how you would feel about it:

Write your Journal Entry Here:

_____

_____

_____

_____

_____

_____

_____

_____

_____

_____

UNIT 12: FREEDOM - William Penn (1644-1718), the Quaker Movement, and Pennsylvania Colony (W12:D1)

Early Years: You know by now that the Americas were named after Amerigo Vespucci, and the Hudson River and many other northern locations were named after Henry Hudson, but did you know that the entire state of Pennsylvania was named after William Penn, who owned the entire state? So how does someone have enough money to own a state's worth of land? What do you have to do to be given that, and then give it away to other settlers - many of whom you don't even know? He did so much more than just give away land.

William Penn was born into a wealthy family, son to a couple from the Netherlands, living in England. His father was an Admiral to the People's Navy during the English Civil War, and was awarded land in Ireland by Oliver Cromwell (taken from Irish Catholics who failed in the Irish Rebellion). After a failed naval mission to take the Caribbean, the Penn family were exiled to their Irish estate. Growing up a Puritan, with a Puritan demeanor, Penn was very strict to the rules. At around 15 years old, his family took in a Quaker missionary to their home, where he learned much of their faith.

When Cromwell died, Penn led the rescue of the exiled Prince Charles, and brought him back to England. As a reward, he was made a Lord over the entire Royal Navy.

While at Oxford, it was acceptable for young men in Penn's position to harass those of lower class and religious minorities; he wouldn't though. He felt a kinship with the often-abused Quakers. For this reason, he would not participate in the activities of others but instead secluded himself to his studies. He began to study the philosophies of economics, politics, and science. Between Oxford firing his mentors, and their increased religious rules, Penn was seen as a rebel and was expelled. This threatened his father's job and mother's social status, so they sent him to Paris to stay.

While in Paris, he stayed with a Protestant theologian. He began to adapt a less strict demeanor of his Puritan beliefs, and replace them with his mentor's belief of free will religion. Two years later, he returned to England and started his short term in college (because, at that time, the Dutch and England went to war). Penn followed in his father's footsteps, joining the Royal Navy. He became an emissary between his father and the King, and when the war ended, his father returned triumphant to a London, though burdened by the Plague, in 1665. During that time, he was sent to care for the affairs of their Irish estate. While away, London burned, in the Great Fire, and upon returning, the city was in a very somber state.

At age 22, he converted to join the Quakers. They had no political leanings, as the Catholics, Protestants, and Puritans all had. They would not pay tithes or swear loyalty to royalty that was not appointed by God. His father was very upset by his son's choices and after trying to reason with his son, ended up throwing him out of the house. Penn moved in with a humble Quaker family, and made friends with George Fox, who started the Quakers. His fight for religious freedom and individualism is said to have extended the Protestant Reformation and began the fight for individual freedom.

Imprisonment

Now, when Penn believed in something, he poured his whole soul- and most of his effort - into it, which made him fit in well with the Quakers, who were known as very loyal to, and pious about, their faith. Now that he was a Quaker, he would use his great writing skills to spread the word, starting with a pamphlet called the *Truth Exalted: To Princes, Priests, and People,* written in 1668, which criticized royalty, church, and state, but mostly all religions excluding the Quakers. He considered it the truest of Christian faiths, in all the Catholic world. His friend and writer, Samuel Pepys, thought the book was "ridiculous". For this act of defiance, and his follow-up book, *The Sandy Foundation*, he was imprisoned and thrown into the tower of London, which housed many Quakers. Bishops wanted Penn imprisoned until he would take back the words written in the pamphlets, but could legally only charge him with publishing without a license. The warrant for his arrest claimed "blasphemy," and was signed by Charles II himself. In his cell, they provided him with pen and paper to recount what he had written, but he immediately wrote another scathing book. After eight months, he was released, though defiant that he would not take back his words.

Over the next few years, thousands of Quakers were imprisoned, and their lands taken by the Crown. Penn was arrested many more times. One of the reasons was his defiance to the 1664 Conventicle Act, in which the government made it unlawful for more than 5 people to assemble outside the family, for any religious purpose, except if you were the Church of England. He was denied seeing the charges, or being allowed to plead his case to the jury who tried him. The jury of his peers, in return, gave him a sentence of not-guilty and when they were pressed to reconsider, they defied the judge and were sent to prison for a few days, to reconsider. The judge threatened the jury with starvation, unless they came back with a guilty verdict. The jury sued the court for their freedom, in what is known as the *"Bushel's Case,"* which was a turning point in London, and allowed all juries to be free from control of the judge.

During his imprisonment, his father was close to death and wanted to meet with his son. William Penn pleaded with his father not to "purchase my liberty," but his father denied his request, so that he could see his son one more time. It is recorded in his father's journals that he had gained a great respect for his son and his faith, that he would stand up for his beliefs, and had grown into a man to be honored. To shield his son one more time, before he died, his father wrote to the Duke of York, heir to the throne, and pleaded for him to protect his son from that time forth. This was the last act of kindness his father could give, and was accepted, because of his service to the Crown.

Upon his father's death, Penn came into a very large inheritance, but this did not sway him from his beliefs, and he was sent to jail, once again. Six months later, after being released, he married his love, after a four-year engagement - which stayed strong even though he was constantly imprisoned. During this time, also, the

Quakers themselves began to divide, due to the philosophies of Penn, versus the founder and mentor of Penn's faith. Because of this, he set off to do missionary work in Germany and Holland.

The Resolution - When he returned, there was such a rift between the Crown and Quakers that Penn proposed a resolution: an emigration of all Quakers - to leave England, for a plot of land in North America. Because of hostilities between the Quakers and Puritans, they could not join any of the other colonies, so he proposed a new colony be started. Penn used much of his inherited wealth, along with other Quakers' wealth, to buy nearly half of what is now New Jersey.

As the Quakers began to move to the area allotted to them, their numbers became too high; Penn pleaded with the Crown to provide them additional land, so more Quakers could emigrate, and the Crown could be rid of these people. Penn purchased another area - the other half of New Jersey and northern Maryland. He also negotiated sovereign rule over the territory, with all rights and privileges. Penn continued to purchase more land that was owned by older noblemen in England, as quickly as possible. The Crown even provided them with more land, and in return, Penn would see that one fifth, the "King's Fifth," of all minerals (gold and silver) were shipped back to the King, and Penn would release the King from the tens of thousands of pounds (English currency) that was owed to him, because of his father.

He first called this land *New Wales*, then changed it to *Sylvania;* but Charles II simply called it *Pennsylvania*. He then turned to do what he did best, and in March of

1681, wrote a charter of Liberties for the entire area - a proto constitution - claiming liberty for the people. Unlike other settlements, he would not allow anyone in his territory to abuse, mistreat, or harm the indigenous people, who still occupied land that was purchased, "As the Lord gave it me over all and great  opposition,... I would not abuse His love, nor act unworthy of His providence, and so defile what came to me clean."

To promote settlers to come, he wrote a number of pamphlets to be spread throughout Europe, promising freedom of religion and beliefs. He attracted many, beyond that of the Quakers, including Huguenots, Mennonites, Amish, Catholic, Lutherans, and Jews from throughout Europe. He quickly returned to the pen, to strip any man too much power, including his own; safeguard free land ownership and enterprise; create a new criminal and justice system, where death sentences were only given to murderers and treason - unlike the hundreds of crimes to be executed for in England; and, instead of being locked in cells until criminals changed, prisons would be a place for rehabilitation. Penn knew the prison and justice systems very well, as he had many run-ins with it in England. He outlawed drunkenness, fighting, cruelty to animals, swearing, and idle amusements, such as gambling.

Much of his philosophy on liberties came from **John Locke,** who spoke against the English ways of ruling over those beneath the Crown. As Penn experienced life in the Americas, he made amendments to his charter of liberties, adding new laws, according to experiences. These laws would need to be passed by the Assembly of elected representatives. He hoped that his amendment process allowed voices to be heard, and would stop rebellion and violence among this territory. Note also, that the Crown had the right, in their agreement with Penn, to override any law he wrote, but his skillful writing made England comfortable with the laws struck. He did see opposition among his own people, as they thought Penn was setting himself up as a ruler.

In 1685 Charles II died, and James, Duke of York, became King. One of his first acts was to protect Penn, as was his promise to Penn's father. Penn, in return, supported the King's actions to regulate Parliament, of which Penn was part. During this time, the colonies were beginning to have serious issues. Penn's lack of attention to detail allowed him to sign a document that gave control of Pennsylvania to Philip Ford, his business manager and fellow Quaker, who, in return, charged Penn a rent, which Penn could not pay. Ford was also found embezzling from Penn's Estate. They came to an agreement, to keep his failings of legal title quiet.

When he returned, he found the territory thriving, with 18,100 settlers - 3,000 of them residing in Philadelphia alone. The economy was thriving, the people were financially stable, and they were relatively happy and at peace. Though there was some opposition, Penn began to open schools to all inhabitants, free to everyone - no matter color or religion, in order to have a well-educated workforce. Philadelphia became the center of the scientific, medical, and psychiatric community.

In his late writings, he wrote about federalizing the other American colonies, and stopping all slavery. Now, Penn had indentured servants and even allowed for debts to be paid through indentured servitude, but he did not support slavery and its injustices. In 1688, during the Germantown Protest, he proposed that all lifetime slaves be freed, after a time of servitude, and that they could live in his proposed Freetown; but the Pennsylvania Assembly rejected the idea. It took the Quakers another 50 years to end slavery. After this rejection by the Assembly, Penn found it his mission to purchase slaves and provide them with good homes. It is said that he cared for all those under his employment. In his will, signed 1701, it was legally binding that "I give to my Servts, John and Mary Sach three hundred acres between them; to James Logan one thousand acres, and my blacks (given) their freedom, as under my hand already; and to ould Sam 100 acres...". In 1758, Pennsylvania (and Quakers alike) abolished all slavery, including indentured servitude.

In 1701, Penn and his wife returned to England, when the French threatened this charter of Pennsylvania. In 1702, Ford died, and his widow, Bridget Ford, threatened to sell all of Pennsylvania, which her husband had embezzled from Penn. She threatened to scrap the Constitution of Pennsylvania. So he tried the only other option, to sell Pennsylvania to the Crown, if they kept the charter of civil liberties Penn had established. Bridget Ford took this matter to the courts in England and Penn landed himself in debtor's prison, charged with unpaid rent to Bridget.

The local Quakers bailed him out. In 1712, more attacks came upon his charter of Pennsylvania, but by this time, Penn was old and frail, and didn't have the stamina to fight. He tried once more to sell the land to the Crown, with his former agreement, but suffered a major stroke. A second stroke left him unable to speak. He died penniless, in 1718. He spent every penny he had to secure the rights of the people of Pennsylvania, including slaves. Those rights would live on to help establish the Declaration of Independence, and the U.S. Constitution.

Activity: Freedom to Believe (Part 1) - This is for you to read, not something to turn in. Write yourself a letter. If you could sum it up in one page, how would you describe what you believe? Write in the letter where this belief came from, and how it started for you. Tell your future self what you believe, and why you believe it. This letter will stay in this book until you pick it up again, sometime in the future. This is for no one else's eyes - only your own.

Dear (State your name) _____

_____

_____

_____

_____

_____

Part #2: In two lines, what did you tell yourself?

_____

_____

What would you do, as an individual, to fight for those freedoms?

_____

_____

_____

Have you ever felt persecuted for your beliefs and how did you overcome that "attack"?

_____

_____

_____

Have you shared them with anyone else? How about your parents? If not, please do. This will only make your beliefs grow stronger, and like Penn experienced, it will garner their admiration.

_____

_____

_____

_____

Women in Exploration (W12:D3) – Sadly, there are few women to report about. Most of the time, the only women that would sail were either pirates, or disguised as men. This was due to both skill and training, at the time, but also superstition that it was bad luck to sail with a woman. Some women found themselves loving the water and would disguise themselves as men; some were found out and those that were not, no one knows about. It is not likely that you would tell anyone after you returned, either, for fear of repercussions.

Filipa Perestrello (1455-1484) the wife of Christopher Columbus, was a noblewoman of wealth, and not from a lower-class family, like Christopher. It is said that their marriage really was not ordinary, but without it, he may never have sailed to the Americas. Who knows?

Anacaona, Queen of Hispaniola (1474 - 1504), was a Taino noblewoman. Before Columbus arrived, the island was divided into five kingdoms. Xaragua was ruled by her husband, until his death, when she took over. Through her influence, there was peace in the land and the Spanish and Taino coexisted, and even intermarried.

In Africa, Alexandrine Tinne (1836-1869) was the first European (Dutch) female explorer to attempt to cross the Sahara Desert. She traveled with her mother and aunt, and though they were halted by death and many failed attempts, were persistent, even up to her death.

In Australia, Jane 'Lady' Franklin (1791-1875), was the wife of John Franklin, a successful explorer of the Arctic. When his expedition disappeared, she supported six expeditions to search for him, finding his frozen body.

Activity: Famous women – What famous women do you know? Do any come to mind that you admire? For example: Madam C.J. Walker, first female, black millionaire; Jane Austin, famous writer; Anne Frank, who harbored Jews during the holocaust; Catherine the Great, who ruled over Russia; Sojourner Truth, American Abolitionist; or Malala Yousafzai, a Pakistani woman who currently fights for women to be educated. These are all great examples and there are so many more. Pick one, and summarize their life below:

_____

_____

_____

_____

_____

_____

_____

_____

Jeanne Baret (1740-1807) – As a French botanist, she sailed with the first French expedition to circumnavigate the world, in 1766, but she had to go in disguise.

Born into a poor family, she took to plants very easily, as her father was a farm laborer and she helped in his chores. Because they were poor, she had no traditional education, but possessed a strong understanding of plant life and medicine. As her full-time work, she became a housekeeper for Philibert Commerson, a medical botanist; she would help him collect his samples, and a friendship grew. Commerson's wife died in 1762. Their friendship grew even more, and she had a child. Because they were not married, she gave the child up for adoption. A French Admiral invited Commerson on his voyage to explore for France, and Commerson said he would join if he could bring his assistant. Because of the law, Jeanne had to disguise herself as a man, and take on the name of Jean.

In 1766, Commerson and Baret set sail on the *Étoile,* to circumnavigate the globe. Commerson and his assistant were given the Captain's quarters, because of the massive amount of equipment and space he needed, which also gave Baret a private bathroom. Baret became the ship's surgeon, out of necessity. All throughout the journey, Commerson and Baret were allowed to leave the ship and collect plant specimens. During much of the voyage, there was a rumor that Baret was a woman, and it is unknown when exactly her gender was revealed. Whatever the truth was, when the ship began to run out of food, near the East Indies in Indonesia, Commerson met with an associate botanist, turned Governor. He stayed on shore as the ship returned to France, and Baret stayed as Commerson's assistant. In 1773, Commerson died and Baret was granted her own property, starting a tavern in town.

In 1774 Baret married Jean Dubernat, a non-commissioned officer in the French Army, who was returning home. By this time, Baret had amassed large wealth, which she brought into the marriage. They sailed back to France together, and in 1785, she was recognized by the government of France to have circumnavigated the globe. Though illegally accomplished, she sued for the recognition and pension that came with it. She and her husband retired and lived long and quiet lives.

Activity: Botany Experiment – Find three plants and draw their leaves in the space below:

What is the difference in each plant?

_____

_____

_____

Journal Entry: Freedom in America: - It can be said that freedom is the greatest feeling life has to give you. Everyone, deep down, wants to be free: free to live your life, believe how your heart dictates, and be who you want to be. Think of how freedom feels to you and write about it in your journal.

Write your Journal Entry Here:

_____

_____

_____

_____

_____

_____

_____

_____

_____

_____

_____

UNIT 13: PIRATES - The Start of Privateering (W13:D1)
Jean Fleury and the Privateers of the European Coast –

 Not much is known of the start of piracy, but it is known that some well-known pirates began as early as the Victual Brothers, or 'Likedeelers,' out of Germany; or the 'Corsairs,' out of France, in the 11th century. To be a privateer, you had to be a private citizen with a warship and given permission from your country's government, by letter, to attack foreign ships and shipments, and return some of the plunder to the country and their crown. This helped pay for their expensive wars, using their enemy's own plunder to rebuild their treasury; some were private ships authorized by the country.

The 'Corsairs' were not part of the French Navy, but were given written permission to attack ships of countries at war with France. Jean de Châtillon, a Catholic bishop in 1144, made the town of Saint-Malo an asylum for pirates, which encouraged all manner of rogues; but by the 13th century, this town progressed into a city of free trade, encouraging commercial activities of craftsmen, merchants, and ship owners, lasting until 1688.

In the 15th century, when rumors were heard of the Spanish sending ships full of gold and treasures back from the New World, the privateers began to salivate. Jean Fleury, and many other privateers – employed by other European nations, besieged these ships and brought their riches back to their native countries.

Activity: Making your Pirate Flag – In the early years of privateering, the ship would fly the flag of the country they stole for, but as treaties were signed and privateering was outlawed, pirates began to sail with their own flags. Here are just a few of the flag flown:

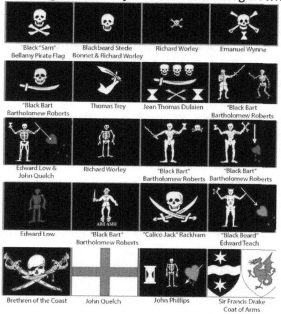

What would your flag look like? Draw it, here:

Jean Fleury (Died in 1527) (W13:D2) - Though his childhood is unknown, he was known to be a skilled pilot in the French Navy, based out of Normandy (off the northern shores of France). Some believe he was born Giovanni da Verrazzano, the French explorer mentioned earlier. When Fleury heard rumors of treasure being shipped from the Americas, he desired his share. As a Naval Pilot and Commander, he controlled a small squadron - 5 ships - and took the responsibility to take this treasure for France. In 1522, **Hernan Cortez** sent three ships from Cuba to Spain, full of treasure from the Aztec Empire. They were sighted close to Portugal, and though Fleury did not know of their cargo, he attacked, laying chase for a few hours before overtaking them.

After overtaking the ships, it was discovered that they were laden with gold from the conquest of Mexico, and were to be presented to **Charles V**, King of Spain. This plunder did not quell Fleury's thirst, for shortly after, he overtook another ship from a Spanish colony on Hispaniola, which also carried tribute. These treasures included exotic animals, food, gold, pearls, jade, and other precious items. A portion of these were sent to Francis I, King of France, as tribute.

The following year, Jean Fleury set sail with eight ships, capturing over 30 Portuguese and Spanish vessels, in just the year 1523. This piracy set off a war between France, Portugal, Spain, and many pirates to come. In 1527, he was captured, tried, and hanged for piracy - on the open ocean. By that time, however, tales of him had spread, and dozens of other pirates in Europe and Caribbean had taken his place, filling their coffers. The Spanish were forced to strengthen their forts, settlements, and ships.

End of the Corsairs and the beginning of free piracy -
Near the end of the 15th century, and as part of a series
of treaties between France and Spain - called the Treaty
of Utrecht, an end was put to the Corsairs, and any
agreements between them and the country of France.
Those who still wanted to be pirates continued their
piracy under the pirate flag, and were hunted down by
the European governments.

Thoughtful Activity: Would you ever become a pirate?
Why or why not?

_____

_____

_____

_____

_____

_____

_____

_____

_____

_____

English Privateers and Pirates of the Caribbean
Sir Admiral Francis Drake (1541 – 1596) (W13:D3) –

Drake was like no other pirate on the open seas. He was an English explorer, sea Captain, privateer, slave trader, naval officer, and politician. He started in humble means, born to a farmer-turned-minister, and became an apprentice to a wealthy merchant. The ship owner was so impressed that, upon his death, he gave his ship to Drake. In 1567, he made his first trip to the Americas, under the command of Captain John Lovell, who took his ships down the coast of West Africa, attacking Portuguese slave cities. They took the plunders, including slaves, to Spanish plantations in the Americas and tried to sell them; in the end, they released over 90 slaves, without payment. In 1568, on his second voyage to the Americas, and while docked at a Spanish fort in Mexico, a fleet of Spanish warships attacked, sinking their ships. Drake and John Hawkins, the owner of the other ship, survived, by swimming away from the rubble. He vowed that day to take revenge on the Spanish.

In 1570, he was provided with two ships, due to his reputation. In 1572, he laid out his plan to sail to Panama and attack the Spanish Galleon ships, full of Incan and Peruvian treasures. His plan was to travel to Tierra Firme - Northern South America - and capture the city of Nombre de Dios, and all its treasures. To do so, he teamed up with the Cimarrons, a group of former African slaves who had escaped, and together, they attacked the city by land and by sea. They captured the city, but as they were finishing off the siege, his men noticed that he was bleeding a great deal, and pleaded with him to withdraw and come back later. They abandoned the treasure, but they stayed in the area and continued to attack the Spanish fleet and plunder their settlements. In 1573, he attacked Nombre de Dios again, by land, capturing nearly 20 tons of gold and silver. They took as much gold as they could carry and buried the rest, then traveled 18 miles to where they had tied up their attack vessels, only to find they had been taken. They buried more of their treasure, built a raft, and Drake floated 10 miles to his flagship, returning days later to pick up his men, as well as their treasure. When he returned to England, England had signed a treaty with Philip II, King of Spain, so Drake couldn't receive any recognition.

One of his accomplishments, while in Panama, was that he climbed a tree at the top of a mountain, and became the first Englishman to see the Pacific Ocean. It was at this point that he wanted to circumnavigate the entire globe. In 1577, Queen Elizabeth I of England gave him his chance. She gave Drake the assignment to fight the Spanish on the western coasts of the Americas. His expedition was patented through King Philip II, but later rejected by him. Drake would take with him Diego - an escaped Spanish slave, who Drake freed after the raid on Nombre de Dios and made his interpreter.

Leaving with five ships, he soon added a sixth, when they captured a Portuguese Merchant ship and employed their Captain, who had experience sailing around South America. During his travels, he lost many ships to rot, battles, and abandonment, when one crew decided to return to Plymouth. Drake continued forward, around The Straits of Magellan and up the west coast of the Americas, laying siege on many Spanish ports and treasure ships, taking their treasures and charts.

He continued north until about Oregon, and returned to California, before sailing west over the Pacific Ocean. Now with a few ships, and burdened with heavy treasures, Drake sought to escape the Spanish by traveling west across the Pacific. He made landfall in the Moluccas Islands, and continued his journey west, around Cape Hope, and arrived back in Plymouth, in September of 1580. Queen Elizabeth soon knighted him on his ship, the *Golden Hind*, performed by a French priest, as she worked to build a stronger relationship with France. Drake became a member of Parliament, working on issues of sailing and the Americas.

As war broke out again, against Philip II of Spain, Drake returned to the sea, attacking Spanish ships. A very large fleet of Spanish warships, known as the **Spanish Armada**, was to leave Cadiz, in 1587, to protect the Spanish treasure ships coming from the Americas; but before they could leave the harbor, Drake and his fleet came swooping into the harbor, early in the morning, and began sinking their ships - somewhere  between 25 to 39 ships (depending on which account you trust - Spanish or English records). This delayed the

Armada's release by an entire year. When they were released, there were still 130 warships that left the harbor for the Atlantic Ocean. During that year, Drake sank another few dozen ships and confiscated their supplies.

When the Armada was released, part of the group was tasked with attacking England and bringing funds to the Spanish troops in the Low Country (also known as the Netherlands). Drake intercepted the fleet and chased them up the channel. At night, he would extinguish all his lights and, under complete darkness (minus one lantern), he captured the Spanish galleon, commanded by Admiral Pedro de Valdes, whose ship carried the gold to fund the continuous war in the Low Country.

In response to the Spanish Armada, Drake was given command of the English Armada, and began hunting the remaining Spanish Armada, especially around Spain and Portugal, which had merged as one country. During this time, he lost many ships to the Spanish and his fleet returned empty handed; in order to boost morale, he attacked the town of Vigo, burning it to ashes. For this, Drake was demoted, and not given another expedition for 6 years.

With this chance, he went back to the Americas and, in several defeats around Puerto Rico, after returning to Panama, he fell ill of dysentery. In his dying breath, he asked that he would be dressed in his royal uniform and buried at sea in a lead coffin. He was dropped into the sea around Portobello, and his coffin has yet to be found, though divers continue to this day to search.

Activity: Mapping Sir Francis Drake's Journey - Reading through his adventures, try to map his journey between Plymouth, the Caribbean, back to Plymouth, down the west coast of Africa, then circumnavigating the globe, and his battles with later Spain.

Activity: Part #2 – Circumnavigating the Globe

How would you have traveled around the world if you had a chance? Name at least two things you would have done differently.

_____

_____

_____

_____

_____

_____

_____

_____

_____

_____

_____

_____

_____

_____

The Golden Age of Piracy (1650 – 1726) (W14:D1)

Piracy came mostly from hatred - caused by the government - against their enemy countries, and the lack of opportunity in their own country. Those countries with money were attacked by those with less; or that was how it was seen, which is why Spain was taken advantage of the most. Most privateers were Welsh, English, Dutch, Irish, and French. They were often private citizens, who commissioned ships to take vessels in the Mediterranean Sea, the Caribbean, Atlantic and Pacific Oceans, coasts of Africa, and all the coasts of Asia; basically, anywhere goods were being shipped, they were tasked with taking their cargo and later selling it in their native countries. Of course, because the government gave them permission, much of their treasure was turned over to royalty, as a commission. When the Kings of Spain and England agreed to a treaty, in 1650, those with permission were no longer allowed to attack their enemies, but were told to stop, yet were not given an alternative. To combat this lack of employment, these ships turned to piracy, and continued to attack their enemy countries' ships and settlements, but now, also turned on their native countries. King Philip I was forced to offer all pirates a pardon, if they gave up their lives of theft, but because of the starvation and unemployment in these countries, there was nothing more for them to do. Many pirates accepted the pardon, but would later return to piracy. There were also loose coalitions of pirates, such as the Brethren of the Coast, who worked together in piracy, until one of them was caught. Most pirates were tried and hung for their piracy and theft, yet their names and legends would continue for years afterwards.

Activity: Time to Bury Treasure – Remember the escape room activity you did earlier? Well, today you will be doing a hunt for buried treasure, and you will be creating a map to help someone find some buried treasure.

Step #1: Find a prize for the players of your game. This could be toys, food, or some other type of prize.

Step #2: Find somewhere hard to find, and place the prize in an enclosed area - where they can't see it in plain sight.

Step #3: Choose a route they will have to take, and put obstacles in their way that they will have to overcome.

Step #4: Draw a map of the classroom or that level of the house, including rooms and the obstacles in them.

Step #5: Create a dot or dash line for the trail they should take, to get from one location to the treasure.

Step #6: Place a big X over the spot where the treasure is, and then give that treasure map to your players. You may need to help them if they can't find their way.

Step #7: Have fun and when it is all done, draw the same map, smaller, in the space below.

Edward Teach "Blackbeard" (1680 – 1718) (W14:D2)–

There is not much known of his childhood, but what is known, is that he was educated in England and could read and write very well. It is speculated that he must have found his way to the Caribbean on a merchant vessel, or slave ship. He is thought to have joined privateer ships throughout the Caribbean, as a crewmember, and fought in the War of the Spanish Succession.

The privateers-turned-pirates, like Henry Jennings, turned a vacant island in the Bahamas into the port of New Providence. It was right in the way of the Spanish shipping lanes, and had a large harbor to house hundreds of ships, but was too shallow for the English and Spanish Navies to attack. This was a floating city without any laws, where only long-term residents lived on land.

After the Treaty of Utrecht was signed, Teach moved to New Providence, as a resident. In 1716, he joined Captain Hornigold, and Captained his smaller ship to capture Spanish ships with thousands of pounds of provisions. On his journey, he came upon Stede Bonnet, a wealthy landowner and military man who turned to piracy and captained a large vessel, the *Revenge*. His men disdained their captain, so they asked Bonnet if Teach could take over. Bonnet relented. Teach's flotilla now consisted of three ships: *Revenge*, his flag ship; his old sloop; and Captain Hornigold's *Ranger*. By this point, Teach began attacking ships and adding them to his army. Hornigold, as a previous British privateer, would not attack his comrades in British ships; so Teach demoted him and he soon returned to New Providence, accepting the King's promised that if a pirate left piracy, they'd be pardoned.

Teach knew the importance of his appearance to his enemies; with a long black beard and black clothing, sometimes his captives recalled him wearing a trench coat with six guns on his chest, and a wide brimmed hat. He took on many names, including those of previous captives to confuse his enemies, but the one name he used mostly was that of Blackbeard. His goal was to strike fear into his enemies. He would not torture or brutalized them, though. Instead, he would ransack their ships, then put the crew back on board and let them go, to tell others of their fearful tale. At the same time, stories came out about him taking the crew of these ships to land, emptying the cargo hull, and burning the ships till they sank into the deep. He is also credited with flying the skull and crossbones, and other similar black flags, used solely to intimidate their enemies.

On November 28, 1717, Blackbeard and two of his ships attacked the French vessel, *La Concorde,* and took it as their own. After repairing the damage they had done to it, Teach renamed the ship *Queen Anne's Revenge*, and made it his flagship, equipping her with 40 cannons. Rumor has it that, at this same time, Teach was waiting near Hispaniola for the Spanish Armada's arrival, where he would take the gold sent to pay the garrison.

In May of 1718, Blackbeard took his flotilla of ships, sailed to the port of Charles Town, in the Province of

South Carolina, and created a blockade of ships, demanding that any ship that passed through be searched and their valuable cargo to be seized. Some of the residents of Charles Town were taken prisoner. Blackbeard's only goal in this blockade was to collect medical supplies and so, he sent one of the ship's Captains back to town to collect them from the port, in exchange for the prisoners. There was a problem, though, for after the supplies were gathered, the pirate escort was found drunk in the nearby tavern, unable to function for a time. The cargo that Blackbeard received was Mercury, which was believed to be a cure for syphilis. He returned the residents almost entirely naked.

After Blackbeard received the medicine, he disbanded the blockade and departed. As the *Queen Anne's Revenge* and his Sloop left, they ran aground, and a plan was dispatched to buy them time. This plan was to test the King's pardon. Blackbeard sent Bonnet to Governor Eden, of the Providence of North Carolina, to ask for a full pardon, which he was granted. Teach was to go next, but when Bonnet returned, he found his men marooned and his ship stripped of its valuables. Bonnet sought revenge against Teach, and they pursued him North. Teach soon showed up in North Carolina and met with Governor Eden for that full pardon, which he was also granted. He was given a commission of privateer against the enemies of the British. The pardon did not last long, as Teach returned to piracy, and a warrant was issued.

In late 1718, Blackbeard took audience with a slew of other notorious pirates, including Charles Vane, Israel Hands, Robert Deal and Calico Jack. They were being pursued by Blackbeard's old companion, Benjamin

Hornigold. The Governors of Pennsylvania and Virginia took notice of this meeting and feared what this would mean, so they sent out warships to capture them. Not trusting the Governors of North and South Carolina, the other Governor commissioned the *HMS Pearl, Jane,* and *Ranger* to capture Blackbeard.

The *Jane* and *Ranger* were sent upriver to find Blackbeard, who was entertaining guests. Most of his crew and guests were on shore at the time. The *Ranger* ran aground, and Captain Maynard, of the *Jane,* commanded his men to attack Blackbeard's ship, the *Adventurer,* by themselves. There, a battle ensued, with Blackbeard's men boarding the *Jane.* Yet, to his surprise, he found that most of the *Jane*'s men were below deck, and when they came from below, the pirates were taken by surprise. Blackbeard and Captain Maynard began a battle with cutlasses, and just as Blackbeard took the upper hand, one of Maynard's men stepped in and mortally wounded Blackbeard. The pirates quickly surrendered, and the battle subsided. Blackbeard's head was taken back to Virginia, to claim the reward money. Blackbeard's crew - on the ship and on land - were captured and shipped back to Virginia. When it was discovered that many of his men were black, Virginians asked for a lesser punishment for them. The men asked to be tried with their comrades and were hanged - all except for Israel Hands, who claimed he was pardoned.

Afterwards, Charles Town, now Charleston, sent out hunting expeditions against other notorious pirates, hanging at least 50 in 1718, alone, displaying their decaying bodies at the entrance of their harbors, to discourage sailors from picking the pirating way of life.

Activity: Pirate Cakes, Hardtack, or Survival Bread

This is a historic mainstay for sailors, pioneers, settlers, and soldiers, when traveling long distances. This is simple and easy, with ingredients that would store for a very long time - even up to a year, if stored correctly. Remember to soak the bread before consuming it.

Ingredients – Hardtack Recipe (Survival Bread)
- 2 Cups – Flour (all purpose flour)
- 3/4 Cup – Water
- 1 1/2 Teaspoons – Salt

Servings: 10-12 biscuits/crackers.

Equipment required: Measuring cup & spoons, mixing bowl, whisk or wooden spoon, rolling pin, spatula, baking sheets, oven mitts, cooling rack, and oven. Preheat oven to 350 degrees F.

Steps to mix and cook:

1) In a bowl, mix the flour, water and salt.

2) Mix until the dough is no longer sticky. Add more flour if it stays sticky (add until the stickiness stops).

3) Spread a little amount of flour on the counter and rolling pin, to keep the dough from sticking. Use the rolling pin to spread the dough out, until 1/2 inch thick.

4) Cut the dough in 3-inch squares. Poke narrow holes in each square, all the way through the top, with a fork or sharp, round item, like toothpicks.

5) Place the hardtack biscuits on a baking sheet.

6) Place the baking sheet into the oven, and bake 25-30 minutes. Use oven mitts to keep from burning yourself.

7) Turn over the hardtack, and bake another 30 minutes.

8) When they are a nice golden brown, take the pan out of the oven. Allow it to cool for 10 minutes on the pan, and then use the spatula to move the biscuits to a cooling rack.

9) Eat immediately afterwards, by soaking it in soup. If you aren't going to eat it right away, place them in an airtight container for longer storage.

Activity Part #2: What did this tell you about the food pirates ate? What does it tell you about the supplies they brought with them?

_____

_____

_____

_____

_____

How would you feel if you had to eat this almost every day? How would you make it taste better, or what type of soup would you have dipped it in to make it taste more appealing? Would you have survived on this diet?

_____

_____

_____

_____

Anne Bonny (1697-1782) (W14:D3) – In 1724, a book  was written about the exploits of two famous women pirates, Mary Read and Anne Bonny. The book was titled, *A General history of the Pyrates.* It was partially fiction, to make it successful, but most came from true accounts of sailing with actual pirates and seeing their lives, including Anne Bonny's crew. Though much of it was fiction, historians took parts of it as truth. So, do we really know what happened? Sadly, no. We also only know what the pirates themselves could report, because most of the time, they would not take prisoners, and those who were on the ships were either hanged and/or were illiterate, so no journals were kept. Historians often like to dramatize a lot of information, mixing fiction with fact, to either prove an agenda, or make the story sound better - though most times, the truth is the greater story. So, let us see what we can piece together of fact, not fiction, but see if fact is just as good.

In the early 1700s, Charleston was a city booming on the North American frontier. It was a young town, growing quickly, by French Huguenot entrepreneurs, merchants, and farmers. It did have its problems, though: pirates. In this town, they were a welcomed bunch; some enjoyed earning their plunder, while others disdained their presence. At this point in time, piracy was legal under English law, and the men were called privateers. In 1713, when the war with France and Spain ended, a treaty was signed, and in it, was a provision to stop all English privateering of French and Spanish ships. Privateers were out of a job, and forced to quit or become pirates. By 1718, this town went from pirate friendly to outlawing every inhabitant that plundered the sea, especially after Blackbeard's blockade. The town had found a new crop (rice), and to be able to ship it to market, they needed a safe route to Europe without Pirates.

Much like other pirates, Anne Bonny's early history is scarce. She is reported to have been born as Ann Fulford, in Ireland, to a servant woman to the lawyer, William Cormac. Not wanting his wife to know that Anne was his, he dressed her up as a boy, called her Andy, and began to teach her to be a lawyer's clerk. When his wife found out that he was raising his illegitimate daughter, she cut his funding. To get away from his wife and her family, he sailed to Charles Town with his servant and her daughter. Cormac was never a successful lawyer (which is why he relied on his wife's family money), so he abandoned his trade and became a merchant, buying and selling goods.

Ann was a beautiful young redhead, with a fiery temper and was known for outbursts of anger. At age 12, her mother died. Just a few years later, she fell in love with James Bonny, a poor sailor and occasional pirate, and married him, only to be disowned by her father and kicked out of the house. In retaliation, it is said that she set fire to her father's plantation, but there is no supporting evidence in Charles Town history. Her husband, seeking a more lucrative pirate career, moved to the Republic of Pirates, New Providence. By that time, many who lived there were former pirates, pardoned by the King, or those trying to hide from the law. The town was not like it used to be, since the treaty was signed between England and Spain. The British had just set up a new government and assigned Woodes Rogers as Governor. James became an informant to the new Governor on pirate activity and gossip. His actions sent many pirates to the hangman's noose. Anne, on the other hand, despised what her husband was doing. She and her husband spent much of their days in taverns, listening to rumors, while she flirted with other pirates to gain their trust. This is where she met John Rackham, also known as "Calico Jack," and fell in love with him. Rackham offered her husband money to divorce her, but he refused and threatened Jack; so, Anne and Rackham ran away, and she became part of Rackham's pirate crew, dressed as a man, again. Only Rackham and another female crew member knew who she really was. That is, until she became pregnant. Rackham then landed her in Cuba, where she divorced her husband and gave birth to a son. A few months later, she rejoined the crew and she and Rackham were married at sea.

A few months after that, Rackham and his two female mates sailed into New Providence (now called Nassau), and stole a ship, releasing their former crewmates to take the other ship. They, in turn, hired a new crew, and spent the next few years in Jamaica and surrounding waters.

In the summer of 1720, their ship was attacked and captured. The Governor of Jamaica had commissioned pirate hunters to clean up waters around the island. Due to most of their crew being drunk, they gave little resistance, and many were hung while still intoxicated. The rest were taken to Port Royal, Jamaica, and stool trial. Both Read and Bonny were held in prison for a time, claiming they were both pregnant. Read was pregnant, but died in prison from fever. As for Anne Bonny, no one knows. There is no record of her release and no record of her hanging. Rackham, on the other hand, was hanged for piracy, along with his crew.

Activity: Alone as Women Pirates - Imagine being only one of two women, in a male dominated world. That is probably how it felt for Anne Bonny in the world of piracy. The pressure on her to perform, and to be as ruthless - if not more - than every other male pirate, must have weighed on her. How do you think this would have felt? If you are male, how would you respond to finding a woman disguised as a man on your ship? If you are female, how would you feel if you were disguised as a man, alone, with an all-male crew? Would it be worth it to sail?

_____

_____

_____

_____

_____

_____

_____

_____

The Witch Trials (W14:D4) – Though this story is not  about pirates, it is about those who were accused of heinous crimes; some may have deserved it, some, not so much. The Witch Trials grew quickly in a literal "witch hunt" throughout all New England colonies. Europe had been searching for witches for generations, spanning well before Columbus sailed to the New World. The search for witches had subsided, in Europe, around the mid 17th century. This is just about the time rumors of witches started to spread in the New World. The first witchcraft execution in the Americas was Alse Young, in 1647, which started the Connecticut Trials. The Salem Trials started in 1691.

Puritans had moved from England to get away from the control of the Crown, but it followed. New England was settled by many different faiths, who left Europe for the same reason. In Massachusetts, they converged, and there was much conflict between them; everything from property lines to church rights was disputed.

Alse Young, the first in the Connecticut Witch Trials – Alse Young was born in 1615, and raised in Windsor, Connecticut. She may have married John Young and had a daughter, Alice. There are no records of a trial for Alse, against the accusation of witchcraft. That same year, 1647, an epidemic of influenza was spreading throughout New England and the death rate was extremely high. Because of everything that was happening. Alse may have been used as the scapegoat, someone to blame for everyone becoming ill, and so was tried off the court records; but her hanging was recorded multiple times. The next year, her husband moved, and possibly changed his name. Thirty years later, her daughter was also accused, but fought it successfully.

Mary Johnson and the first confession – Mary was a house servant and was accused of theft, in 1648. After being interrogated, and even tortured, she stated that she had "familiarity with the devil," that she had relations with men and the devil, and even murdered a child. No evidence was collected to prove these claims, and her execution was delayed until she gave birth. She was executed on June 6, 1650.

Elizabeth Hubbard, Accuser in the Salem Witch Trials – Elizabeth was a 17-year-old orphan, who became the maidservant to her uncle, Dr. William Griggs. She and a group of friends, headed by Abigail Williams and Betty Parris, began accusing others of witchcraft, after being found playing with the like. When questioned, the two would start having fits, contortions of their bodies, and screaming. Elizabeth's fits started the next year. Dr. Griggs examined the girls to find nothing wrong with them, and claimed that it had to be supernatural. Elizabeth was 18, by then, and could testify in court, unlike most of the other girls. She began accusing more and more colonists of witchcraft and sending the girls into fits. Her last testimony (of the 32 times it was given, with more than 40 accusations) was in 1693. These accusations resulted in 17 arrests, 13 hangings, and two dying while in jail. After the trials, she disappears from records, which may be due to her changing her name.

Dorothy Good: the four-year-old witch – Dorothy and her mother were accused of practicing witchcraft, in 1692. Dorothy was interrogated by the local magistrate and even "confessed" to seeing her mom talking with the devil. Two of Hubbard's cohorts claimed the child had bit them, as if like an animal. Dorothy was sent to jail. She made many interesting comments but was still released months later, on bond. She never stood trial.

Mary Bliss Parsons – Mary Bliss Parsons was born in England, in 1628, and immigrated to Connecticut, around 1646. She met Joseph Parsons, and they married the same year. In 1655, they moved to Massachusetts and purchased land from the local tribe, to help start the town of Northampton. They were very successful, owning land throughout Massachusetts.

In the 1650s a feud developed between the Parsons and a neighboring family, the Bridgmans. While the Parsons were successful and healthy, the neighbors were quite the opposite. Rumors began to spread that the Parsons were causing cattle to die, and that Mary had cursed their son. She was called a witch, and the rumors spread. In 1656, Joseph Parsons brought the matter to court and sued the Bridgmans for slander. The court sided with the Parsons and ordered the Bridgmans to apologize. In 1674, they again charged Mary Parsons with witchcraft, after their daughter suddenly died. The local magistrate searched Mary's body for witch-marks and then decided to ship her to Boston and that court sided with Mary. Though the courts were convinced, the rumors of Mary being a witch spread everywhere they moved. Her husband died in 1683. She lived, suffering from the same rumors, for the next 30 years, until she died.

John Proctor – John was born in England and immigrated to Massachusetts with his wealthy parents, at three years old. He became a successful businessman and had four children. His wife died in childbirth to the only child to survive childhood. Three years later, he married Elizabeth Thorndike, and moved to Salem, in 1666. They had seven children; five survived. She died in 1672. In 1674, he married Elizabeth Bassett and had another seven kids; five of these also made it to adulthood. By now, Elizabeth and the older kids ran their tavern.

In 1692, rumors spread about Elizabeth being a witch. When Proctor stood up for her, he was accused, too. His accuser was Abigail Williams, one of Hubbard's cohorts. Hubbard brought these accusations to court with a petition in his favor, signed by 32 neighbors. The Proctors were tried on August 5, 1692, found guilty, and sentenced to death by hanging. While they were in jail, their property was stripped by the local sheriff and sold. The children were left with nothing. Rumor is, that he was given a chance to confess, to save himself from hanging, but he would not lie by signing his name. John was hanged on August 19, 1692. Elizabeth's hanging was delayed, because she was pregnant. She was eventually released.

In the end, 141 complaints were filed against John, Elizabeth, and other family members - even his children. When Elizabeth was finally released, all their property was gone, and the courts would not even recognize her as living for the next seven years. Together, all those accused, and their family members, filed petitions to reverse the courts. In 1711, the government finally reversed the convictions, and they were awarded money for the property the local government had stolen.

George Burroughs – George was born in England and then moved to be raised by his mother, in Massachusetts. He graduated from Harvard and became a pastor, to preach in Salem, in 1680. A conflict started between him and his congregation when they weren't paying his wages. In 1681, when his wife died, he borrowed money from John Putnam, a community member, to pay for her funeral. When he couldn't pay Putnam, he resigned and left Salem. He moved to Maine, until his town was destroyed by the Wabanaki in 1690.

While in Wells, Maine, he was accused of witchcraft, by those he owed money. He was accused of many other things, also, including mistreating his accusers, ten years previously. He was hanged - the only minister to be executed during the trials. While waiting, with the rope around his neck, he recited the Lord's prayer, which was said to be "impossible for a witch."

The Aftermath - In the end, the majority (78%) of those executed were women. The trials and processes to try a witch were set up by the Court of Oyer and Terminer. It convened, for the first time, in Salem, on June 2, 1692, with Bridget Bishop being the first to be tried and executed. Things were getting out of hand, and innocent people were being executed. This information made its way to Governor Phips, who was fighting in Maine. He declared that the trials must stop. After seven months of trials, and many executions, the Superior Court met, to find nearly everyone accused not guilty. The trials finally ended in April 1693. Everyone still alive was released. Those who survived petitioned - for years - to overturn the convictions of all accused, including the 19 executed, the five who died in jail, and the one crushed.

Activity: Let's Play Accusation – Is it fun to be accused of something you didn't do? Here is a little activity to help you know how it feels. This is to be played in the classroom, with your class, or at home with your family. Everyone sits in a circle or around a table. Cut small, equal sized pieces of paper, enough for each person to get one. Write "ACCUSED" on one piece. Place all the papers in the middle of the table, or in a container, (folded in half, so no one can know which paper is picked). Everyone grab a piece and without anyone seeing, look at your paper. The person who was the first to pick up "ACCUSED" is automatically not accused; instead, they will be the "ACCUSER." Place the paper back into the container and have everyone pull out another piece. Do this five times, so at least five people are accused. Mark it in the book, in the space below, if you are accused (use one rectangle to record each time you receive the "ACCUSED" paper, each game). After five times, put the paper back in the container and hold up your fingers, showing how many times you were accused. Those who were accused, then get to guess who the accuser is (which was the first person that round to draw the "ACCUSED"). If you pick the right person, you win. Play this game as many times as you like.

1.	2.
3.	4.
5.	6.
7.	8.

Journal Entry: Privateering and Piracy in Americas: - Now, a few days back, we only gave you a taste of what pirate life would have felt like: attacking other ships, plundering for your country, being hunted by other ships, and living your life as a criminal and outlaw to be hunted and killed. Now reflect on what pirates, 300-400 years ago, might have felt, and write about it in your journal. If you so choose, substitute pirates for those accused of witchcraft, and write about how they may have felt:

Write your Journal Entry Here:

_____

_____

_____

_____

_____

_____

_____

_____

_____

_____

UNIT 15: MISSION – Catholic Missions (W15:D1)

One of the missions of exploring the Americas, for Spain and Portugal, even back to the time of Columbus, was to spread Catholicism and Christianity to the New World. In the beginning, Spain would send one or two priests to the Americas on each ship, then many began to sail to this new land by the dozens. These priests would set up settlements of faith, called missions, everywhere Spain and Portugal claimed, including all lands between modern-day Mexico, to Argentina, in the most Southern tip of South America, and even some parts of North America, such as Florida, Georgia, and Texas. Some priests would go further, living among the indigenous people, teaching them, and even protecting them from other European explorers (as well as their own countrymen). There was respect given to priests and faith-based settlements, so while other nations would attack Spanish settlements, most of the time, missions were held in higher regard,as being sacred. Pirates did not always hold them in such high esteem, though.

But missions were not just for the Americas. Many were started in Asia and Africa, as means of conversion, and some ecclesiastical and political matters. The Catholic priests and missionaries worked with the royal courts in China to foster relations and increase trade with Spain and Portugal. Catholic missions were set up throughout West Africa, though under great threat by Muslim rulers. The priests and missions in Northern Africa, because they were religious institutions, were not often attacked, as much as they were pressured by the local rulers to leave. Those in the south, where Muslim rulers had less control, were less likely to feel the hostility from the locals, and thrived in that area. Some of the Jesuits were sent to minister unto the white Christian slaves, sold in the African slave markets. João Nunes Barreto was a Portuguese Jesuit who was assigned to Africa, between 1548 and 1554, to minister to these white Christian slaves. He returned to Europe, in 1554, to raise funds to buy their freedom; instead, he was named Patriarch for Ethiopia, and was not able to return to free them all. The Portuguese Jesuits set up entire villages throughout modern-day Angola and taught the natives in that area. The tribes would join their cities to find work and learn, including children and slaves.

In 1508, Pope Julius II, *Universalis Ecclesiae (Of the Universal Church)*, declared that the King of Spain would head the Church in Spain, and its empire. Soon after, the King declared "Patronato Real," or Royal Patronage, which gave Spain absolute control over ecclesiastical - church related - matters within their empire. The document also gave the Spanish the responsibility of promoting conversion, education, civilizing, and keeping the indigenous people safe from being harmed by Spanish or other exploration. They were also responsible for building churches, convents, hospitals, and schools, throughout the Americas. This patronage also provided the Crown with more money to spend, including increased taxes among settlers, explorers, and merchants, to provide for their missions.

The missions themselves were not always large churches or compounds; they were as simple as a single hut in the middle of a tribal village, as close to the Chief's dwelling as possible. They were tasked with being the servant of the tribe, in matters dealing with the Spanish explorers, and all matters to do with the faith of the indigenous people. For villages that were spread out, they would construct a central compound, where they could hold mass and be centralized to move among the many villages. The Chiefs enjoyed becoming part of the mission system, because they were given deep respect by the Spanish, and were provided gifts and clothing that were traded by the Spanish.

In some cases, the Chiefs would provide workers for Spanish settlements, who would work among the settlers to farm the land, teach them how to farm, and build great buildings. **St Augustine**, Florida, reports that nearly 300 mission Indians were drafted by the Chiefs to work in the settlements between March and September, being paid an agreed-upon wage. Because the Chief drafted them, there was less conflict among the tribe and the Spanish. Sadly, their interaction with the Spanish caused disease to spread among the native workers, and sometimes even back to their villages.

Franciscan missionaries – The Franciscans were the first organized group to arrive in New Spain (modern-day Mexico), just after Cortez's conquest over the Aztecs and Mexico. They were assigned to Mexico, Texcoco, and Tlaxcala. Their task, beyond conversion, was to teach all natives the skills that they deemed necessary, including reading and writing Spanish, and adult skills, such as carpentry, ceramics, and metallurgy. Pedro de Gante was one of the first to arrive in New Spain and saw some of the culture as needing a change, including ritualistic killing of their enemies. To help them change, he took the tactic of assimilating himself into their culture and influencing them from within. He learned their language and culture, and even participated in their games and other activities. He also worked to educate their youth and adults, and gained the trust of the people. It was then that he slowly showed them a different way to act. His classes were recorded to be as large as 600 indigenous children. His influence and success spread wide throughout the Franciscan community, and others took up the same methods of assimilation. By 1532, nearly 5,000 children were educated throughout all of New Spain. Because the friars believed that conversion, among the indigenous people, should be done by meditation and free will, which took longer, the Spanish Crown believed it was not happening fast enough. The local governments claimed that the friars were mistreating the people. In return, the friars began to report that the Spanish were enslaving the people, and mistreating the natives. Pressure from the Spanish crown made many friars flee, traveling west to other tribes they could help. The Franciscan parishes were almost all dismissed.

The Jesuit Order in America (1570-1767) – After the fall of the Franciscan order in New Spain, the Jesuit priests arrived, around 1570. They set up missions (they called Reductions), to better control, convert, and protect the indigenous people. In these missions, the indigenous people were given a home and land to farm. They would then collect all crops, and return them to the mission. In return, the Jesuits would distribute food and clothing to them. These people were used to build churches, schools, and hospitals. Two Jesuits were tasked to manage the workers and the local native leaders. This was a very feudalistic (or socialistic) system, where the few controlled the distribution of goods to the masses.

Before the Jesuits were expelled from Mexico, there were over 140,000 Indians working in these farms and 1732 Reductions spanning throughout the Americas.

The Dominican Order (W15:D2) - Bartolomé de las Casas was the first Dominican Bishop in Mexico. He came to Hispaniola as the son of a merchant, during Nicolás de Ovando's expedition. Remember, it was Ovando who was to investigate and eventually arrest Columbus's successor, the second Governor of Hispaniola, for lying to the crown about Columbus and his mistreatment of the Taino people. This was Las Casas's first experience with mistreatment of the indigenous people. When Ovando took control and began to turn the territory around, this behavior fascinated Las Casas. Las Casas was given land of his own, to farm and mine, and used native slave labor to do so, even participating in slave raids and military expeditions against the natives.

In 1510, he became a priest, and joined a group of Dominican friars who had just arrived in Santo Domingo. They saw the atrocities caused by the Spanish and began to deny confession to the slave owners. Las Casas was one of those denied Confession. He argued with the friars as to the need for "encomienda" - the practice of giving those who helped conquer land their own "property" of land and slaves. Diego Columbus sent a complaint to the King about the Dominicans, and they were recalled from Hispaniola. They were then dispatched to other Spanish areas in the Americas.

When Las Casas accompanied the Spanish during the Conquest of Cuba, his perspective began to change. He wrote: "I saw here cruelty on a scale no living being has ever seen or expects to see". This did not stop him from receiving more land and slaves through encomienda, though. His land produced much gold and riches for him. According to his biography, it was the study of Ecclesiastes, in the Bible, that finally opened his eyes.

From that point forward, he renounced slavery, and encomiendas, and became an activist for indigenous people's rights, and started to criticize the Spanish greatly for their atrocities. He began writing letters advocating bringing in African slaves, to reduce the suffering of Indian slaves (which, later in life, he retracted, when he began to see the error of using African slaves, as well). He initially desired to stop the harsh treatment of the indigenous people, and not the act of slavery - not until his later years. He even traveled back to Spain to convince the King to end encomiendas.

The problem was that those in charge of these matters were also receiving encomiendas. His audience with the King was never granted to him and Ferdinand later died without meeting him. Ferdinand's successor, Prince Charles, was too young to be bothered with these matters, and so, after hearing from Las Casas, Cardinal Cisneros sent a group of monks to take control of the islands and stop the harsh treatment of the indigenous people. These monks stripped a few of the encomiendas from those who were not living on the land, including a Bishop who owned land, but lived in Spain. These monks decided that the natives were incapable of living on their own, and so allowed the encomiendas to continue. Las Casas was furious and disbanded the commission. The Spaniards began to despise Las Casas, for trying to destroy their way of life, and he had to seek refuge with the Dominicans for fear of death. By 1517, Las Casas was forced back to Spain.

None of these failed attempts stopped Las Casas, and he continued to work to promote a free indigenous people. The Dominicans were not only attacked by the Spanish, but were also under attack by other native tribes, such as the Caribs, who were sworn enemies of the Taino. The Caribs were provoked by the Spaniards, conducting slave raids on the native villages and taking more of their people as slaves. The Caribs saw themselves as being allowed to make these raids, but not when it came to their people being taken. When the Caribs attacked the missions, they would massacre everyone, including women and children. Las Casas's enemies used this massacre in the Dominican mission to garner military support. The Nuevo Laws of 1542 established the disbanding of encomiendas; only, after the owner died, the crown would gain possession of the land, and all slaves would be released. This gradual abolition of indigenous slavery began to foster the need for more African slaves, and this empowered slave traders.

There was more opposition in New Spain. Riots started, and threats were made against Las Casas's life. Even the Viceroy of New Spain, who benefitted from encomiendas, decided he would not follow the law to abolish the encomiendas. Las Casas was not liked in the Americas, and when the Nuevo laws were repealed in 1545, riots broke out again. Colonists tried to take Las Casas's life, forcing him to move back to Spain. He would write books and letters recounting the history of New Spain, that were sometimes refuted, but his desire was only to set the people free in the New World.

Activity: Abolishing Slavery — Say you were a slave owner and your entire livelihood was dependent on using indigenous slaves. Then one day, you decided that slavery of natives was evil and wrong. What would you do? What could you do, considering your farm would collapse without slaves to farm your land?

_____

_____

_____

Now, consider a law was passed that said any native freed would then be recaptured and enslaved, if you freed them? What would you do?

_____

_____

_____

Lastly, consider you were given an alternative to use slaves from another country, and these slaves were not against the law to keep. What would you do?

_____

_____

Exploring Texas and the West (W15:D3) – In 1519, Captain **Alonso Alvarez de Pineda** was given a secret commission: to take on Cortez and bring him back for trial, before he could attack the largest indigenous civilization in Mexico. His cover was a mission to map the entire Gulf Coast, from Florida to Mexico. While mapping the coast, he would conduct a few expeditions inland, being the first European to set eyes on Texas. After failing to capture Cortez, he returned, to try and establish the first fort in Texas, but the Huastec Indians attacked and killed everyone, all their horses, and burned everything to the ground.

In 1528, **Alvar Núñez Cabeza de Vaca**, along with three Conquistadors (one being from Africa, named Estevanico), was commissioned to explore the lower portion of North America. In 1530, their ship was wrecked on the coast of Texas. Those that survived were forced to walk, making it as far as Mexico, by 1536. Vaca was rescued by the **Karankawa** tribe and lived with them for many years. After he left, the tribe had no contact with Europeans, until 1685, when the French built Fort Saint Louis.

In 1540, Francisco Vázquez de Coronado was ordered to explore, from the west, more of Southwest North America and made it as far as New Mexico, among the Pueblo Indian tribe. The tribe had heard from others how to deal with European explorers and sent them on a wild goose chase in search of gold, across northern Texas, Oklahoma, and Kansas. At the same time, Luis de Moscoso Alvarado explored from the east, coming west from the Mississippi River, and made it as far as central Texas, before returning home.

Though there were many explorers who traveled across Texas, there was no supply route, until Juan de Oñate was commissioned to develop the Pueblo Indians' land, and create a supply route into that land. From there, missionary and trade activities began to flourish. Fray Juan de Salas was called upon by the Jumano Indians, for religious instruction, and lived there, among the people, with his other friars.

In 1681, the indigenous of the area rebelled against the Spanish and drove them southward, to the El Paso area. They returned and built fortified missions, including Corpus Christi de la Isleta and Nuestra Señora del Socorro, the first Spanish settlements in Texas.

The French, commanded by René Robert Cavelier (Sieur de La Salle), tried to claim the Mississippi area in 1682. Being that they already came from the north, by land, into the Louisiana region, this time, they wanted to claim it by sea. The first expedition explored the Mississippi River, while the second expedition overshot the River and ended up 400 miles further west, in Texas. They were short on supplies because two ships were lost at sea, but they made landfall and established Fort Saint Louis, several miles inland. In 1687, during an expedition away from the fort, La Salle was murdered by his men.

In 1689, the Spanish sent a group, including Captain Alonso de Leon, the Governor of parts of Texas, to confront the French. All they found were the ruins of what was Fort Saint Louis. Indians had attacked the fort, driving survivors east, further into Texas; they were never found.

Father Damián Massanet accompanied Leon on an expedition to find survivors. He was fascinated with the Tejas (meaning "Friendly") Tribe. The Tejas were part of the **Caddo Confederacy** of tribes that lived in Texas, Louisiana, Arkansas, and Oklahoma. The Caddos believed in one God and when the friar introduced Christianity to them, the tribe asked him to stay and set up a mission to instruct them. The Spanish government lost interest when they heard the French were no longer a threat in the area, and withdrew support. The Tejas were also struck by an epidemic, because their immune systems were not used to European diseases. The tribe blamed the new religion and felt they were being cursed; they began to resist. In 1693, the mission was closed and they withdrew from east Texas.

In the end of the 1600s, the Spanish introduced horses to the area. The Apache used them to expand their territory to the lower Texas Plains, taking over the traditional hunting grounds of the Jumanos (nomadic settling area of the Coahuiltecan), and territory of other tribes. Texas would never be the same, as the Spanish and Indian relationships entered the 1700s.

During the 1600s, the Spanish interacted with over seventeen different tribes, throughout Texas, who were hospitable and friendly. Most of these tribes no longer exist today, due to either European disease or territorial tribes attacking and destroying the less aggressive tribes.

A driving goal of the Spanish exploration in Texas was to find gold and other precious treasures. Yet, they never found them, which is why the Spanish government didn't see Texas as a viable use of their funds.

Activity: Traveling in the Unknown – Today is the day to face your fears, and go where no student has gone before. Today, you are to find a large room in your school, house, or other location, and black out the windows with large shades or construction paper (ask permission, first, of course). You want this room to be able to be near pitch black. Your next task is to set up obstacles throughout the room or, for more fun, have someone else set up these obstacles for you. Your task is to make it from one point in the room to another location in the room, with all the lights off. You want to experience the fears and excitement of the Spanish as they explored this new territory of Texas. They had no idea what to expect; they just knew what their goal was, and hoped for the best. Now, it's your turn.

After your expedition into the dark
How did you feel walking into the dark?

_____

Did you walk through perfectly, or make mistakes?

_____

How do you think the Spanish felt exploring?

_____

_____

Journal Entry: Missionary Life – Missionaries in the Americas had many jobs. They were not just about teaching their faith, but also teaching the indigenous people, writing down the history and culture of the people, searching out mistreatment, and teaching the settlers who traveled to this new country. If you were coming over from Europe as a missionary, what would your first priority be with your mission? Reflect on it for a little bit, and then answer this question in your journal.

Write your Journal Entry Here:

_____

_____

_____

_____

_____

_____

_____

_____

_____

_____

UNIT #16: SLAVERY – Comes to America (W16:D1)

With the Nuevo Laws of 1542 in full swing, and the encomiendas being abolished, the Spanish needed to find other forms of labor. So they turned to the African slave markets. In Africa, African civilizations - like those of Mali - would attack neighboring villages, and entire countries, to take the land and property, and then force those captured into slavery. They would gather the people, tie them to each other (to prevent an individual from running), and march them into their slave markets, to be sold to the highest bidder. Those that purchased these slaves were from all over the world; nearly every nation purchased and sold slaves at some point in their history. The Muslim civilizations in Africa were the first (and largest) merchants of slaves in all the world, selling black, white, and tan slaves. If they were captives and could be sold, it didn't matter who they were. Some merchants would take slaves from one market and sell them to other markets, such as African markets to European, Asian, or American markets. They would march them to their destination, or load them onto ships, like livestock. Many died while being transported and their bodies would be thrown to the side of the road or into the sea. Those shipped to the Americas were loaded into slave ships, crammed to allow very little movement, in order to transport as many slaves as possible.

The **Transatlantic Slave Trade** started in Hispaniola, the Caribbean islands, and all the Spanish colonies in the islands. This then spread to the Spanish and Portuguese colonies all throughout South America. The Portuguese, in Southern Brazil, are recorded to have bought and sold

21% of all slaves that were shipped over the Atlantic, second to Spain's colonies in Jamaica, at 11% of slaves.

John Hawkins, a British privateer, was commissioned to attack Spanish ships in the open ocean, and begin **Triangle Trade** between England, Africa, and the Americas. In 1562, he set sail for Africa, purchasing and capturing 300 slaves. He then took them to plantations in the Caribbean and South America. He took the money and treasures he traded them for back to England, to present them to Queen Elizabeth I, who was very pleased and commissioned him to continue. She also awarded him a Coat of Arms, with the images of slaves on it. His second cousin, **Sir Francis Drake**, who accompanied him on his first few slave trading missions, ended up denouncing slavery, and turned to piracy when the crown called a truce with Spain. He would end up partnering with escaped slaves to attack the Spanish. When he captured a city, he would free the slaves, including the Turks, in Colombia.

In Puritan, Huguenot, Protestant, and Quaker run North America, African slaves were not sold into lifetime slavery, for it was against the law. Instead, they were limited to four to seven years of servitude, and then had to be released. In 1526, in the San Miguel de Gualdape colony, in South Carolina, a slave ship arrived from the Caribbean to sell slaves. There was an uproar, and the slaves were released, fleeing to find safety among the local native tribes. The law stated that lifetime slavery was not permitted. In 1565, Don Pedro Menendez de Aviles brought his slaves, when he moved from the Caribbean, to build the Spanish fort of St. Augustine, Florida.

Now, indentured servants were allowed in the colonies, as most settlers could not afford to pay the fees to travel to the New World. They, in turn, would promise an amount they would work, normally four to seven years, to pay their debt for the trip. Most of the colonies wrote laws against slavery, but there were those in the South who conducted slave raids on Native American villages, enslaving up to 24,000 Native Americans. Again, this was against colonial law and, if found that this was done in lands where it was against the law, the owners would be imprisoned, and the slaves released.

In 1601, after the Battle of Kinsale, the British captured

30,000 Irish military prisoners. The Thirty Year War had left England in major debt. Both during the rule of James II and **Oliver Cromwell** (1649-58), they pushed to sell the Irish into servitude throughout the Americas, especially in Barbados and other Caribbean islands, to fill their treasury again. See, this was forced servitude; the English would sell the Irish to slave traders, in exchange for products from the Americas, like cotton and tobacco (and then sell those), but they were to be freed after seven years. They were also threatened that, if they returned to Ireland, they would be sold back into servitude. In 1612, the first Irish servants are recorded to have been sold to a settlement on the Amazon River. In 1625, an official Proclamation ordered Irish prisoners to be sold to English Planters in the Americas. By 1637, 69% of Montserrat were Irish servants. The Irish, at that time, were the largest source of forced labor in the English slave markets. Between 1641 and 1652, under Oliver Cromwell's rule, nearly 550,000 Irish were killed and 300,000 more sold into slavery. Irish servants were mostly men, stripped from their families because the English could get more money for them. In the 1650s Irish children were also found to be profitable, and so were taken away from their Irish Catholic families and sold as servants in Virginia, New England, and the West Indies. Historians report that, until 1650, there were more European indentured servants sold in the Americas than slaves from Africa. Europeans also "cured" their Romanichal Gypsy overpopulation issues by selling them in the Americas, as indentured servants.

In 1619, British privateers attacked and captured a Portuguese cargo ship, the *White Lyon*, heading for Brazil. They needed to sell their cargo, including African slaves, and so made their way to Jamestown, Virginia. Because of North American colonial laws, people could not be sold as slaves, but rather servants, like the Irish. These 20 Africans, including families, were sold into servitude and given the same rights as white servants, and were to be released after seven years. In 1640, John Punch, an African servant, tried to escape his service and the courts ruled to make him the first servant-for-life. In

1654, John Casor, another African indentured servant, pleaded with the courts that he had served his time for his master, Anthony Johnson (who was also a freed African servant). Casor, and a few white settlers, won his first court appearance against his master, but Johnson appealed the decision and won the appeal, making Casor the first lifetime slave without a criminal conviction in North America. This ruling stripped all rights that had been given to blacks in America before this time.

In 1672, King Charles II gave the monopoly of all African trade in the British colonies to the Royal African Company. By 1676, Parliament made slave trading in British colonies legal, overriding the laws that were established in the colonies, by the colonists. The British colonies account for 4% of the Transatlantic Slave Trading. By 1730, other traders had broken through the monopoly, to begin selling slaves in North America.

It was not only the south that enslaved Africans. It is reported that, at one point, 42% of New York City households employed slaves from Europe and Africa, inside their residence. The northern colonies were more likely to make slaves servants inside their homes, while the south made them labor in the hot fields, farming their crops. The African slave trade was the  only thing allowing the south to succeed, as there was not enough labor to farm the land with crops like rice, cotton, tobacco, etc. When a slave gave birth, that child was raised for a time, and then sold into slavery, as well. This resulted in the colonies depending less on slaves coming from Africa, and more on those who were born into slavery.

In the south, the new colony of Georgia was established in 1733. In 1735, the Georgia Trustees created a law to stop all slave trade in Georgia. At this point, slavery was legal in all other British colonies. This was one of the first attempts to fight back against British governance in the colonies.

In French-owned Louisiana, King Louis XIV wrote into law the *Code Noir*, which gave specific rights to slaves, including the ability to marry. It forbade torture, and did not allow slave masters to separate couples. It required the owners to teach their slaves in the way of the Catholic faith. Future laws also allowed those born to slave mothers and white fathers freedom from slavery. These children were to be educated and allowed to own property, businesses, and even their own slaves. The *Code Noir* outlawed interracial marriage among whites and blacks, but this did not stop the people.

Activity: Simulated Servitude - Today, you will participate in a simple assignment. You will give yourself a small perspective/opportunity to see what being a servant felt like. You will give yourself to another student or family member, and act as their servant for a day. For this experiment, that person may not hurt you or do anything that you would not do before this activity, much like servants had to experience, but you must serve them the entire day.

What did you feel acting as an indentured servant for someone?

_____

_____

Did they have you do anything you did not want to do?

_____

_____

What were some of the chores you had to do for them?

_____

_____

_____

_____

Actual Servitude: We only gave you a taste of what servitude would have felt like, without the abuse and harsh conditions. Now, reflect on what actual servitude - back a few hundred years ago - would have felt.

How might they have felt, as a servant for 4-7 years?

_____

Did they have them do anything they did not want?

_____

What were some of the responsibilities they had to do?

_____

_____

Would you have tried to escape if you were either a servant or slave to someone for many years to life?

_____

_____

_____

_____

_____

Eleanor 'Nel' Butler (1665-???) (W16:D2) – At a very young age, Eleanor Butler was stripped from her parents in Ireland, and shipped - by the English government - to Maryland, to be sold into Indentured Servitude. This means that she would need to serve for 7 years, if she hoped to receive her freedom. A man by the name of Charles Calvert, 3rd Baron of Baltimore, purchased her to work in his home. At age 16, she announced her intentions to marry "Negro Charles" an African American slave. Maryland law claimed that a "free" woman who voluntarily married an enslaved man would serve his master until his death, and any child born, into slavery.

Lord Baltimore became distressed by this, that a white woman would be enslaved, or that his friend Calvert may lose a servant to a slave owner, so he petitioned the Provincial Assembly to change the law, and in 1681, key parts of the law were changed. Now, it was against the law for female servants and male slaves to be married, and fines were to be placed on the master.

Eleanor did not care, and married Charles anyway, before the law went into effect. William Boarman became her master. They had eight children, each born into slavery. One of their sons ran away and later purchased his freedom from the Boarmans.

It wasn't until 1770 that two of their grandchildren, William and Mary Butler, who were still enslaved, sued for their freedom, on the basis that they were descendants of a white woman. It took them until 1787 to petition the court enough to set them free, because the courts did not want their decision to affect slave owner's "property."

Amos Fortune – With most slaves, there is very little  record of their childhood - simply that they were born in Africa, and captured, sold, and shipped to the Americas. Fortune's story has a similar start. The first record of his existence is his "freedom papers," signed by his former owner, Ichabod Richardson, on December 30, 1763. Fortune helped in a tanning shop in Massachusetts Bay. This gave an agreed upon deadline of when he would be freed: in four years. When Richardson died abruptly, in 1768, there was no mention of Fortune's release. He instead made a new agreement with Richardson's heirs to buy his freedom, making his final payment in 1770.

After buying his freedom, he continued to live in Massachusetts Bay, working for other landowners, until he could purchase his own land and house, with the help of Richardson's heirs. He also purchased the freedom of a woman named Lily Twombly – whom he married. Sadly, she died less than one year later. In 1779, Fortune purchased the freedom of another woman, Violet, and they were married and soon adopted a slave child.

In 1781, Fortune moved to establish his own tanning company, and then bought another 25 acres. His company prospered and he was well-known and liked among the residents of the area. He even employed many apprentices to help. He died in 1801, at age 91; Violet died in 1802, and was buried next to him.

Bacon Rebellion (W16:D3) – In the early 1650s, the Northneck Frontier (or Western Virginia) was not well populated.  The colonists began to spread out into this area, while the larger native tribes did the same, including the Chicacoan, Doeg, Patawomeck, and Rappahannock. Colonists did not like the competition, and in 1699, declared war on the tribes. By 1670, they pushed most of the Doeg out of the colony of Virginia.

Trying to pressure Governor William Berkley (a veteran from the English Civil War) out of Jamestown, Nathaniel Bacon (Berkeley's cousin and a member of the court) started a rebellion among other colonists, which grew like a wildfire. Bacon had many different demands, including British pricing of goods, among other things, but the most well-known cause was that of defending against natives in frontier land. He wanted to force them out of colonial territory. Berkley, on the other hand, wanted to keep those around that he could use as spies, intelligence, and labor. Some also call the native struggles a scapegoat to focus on, instead of the economic issues that plagued the colonies at the time. Many tribes were conducting raids on the frontier farms.

Berkeley promised to investigate the matter, and during a meeting with both sides, a battle broke out. Some tribal leaders were killed. Berkeley needed to bring peace quickly, and wanted to work together on a peaceful solution, so he stripped the Indians of all powder and ammunition for a time - an act the Indians were not happy about. More raids were launched.

To show the strength of the rebellion, Bacon gathered thousands of Virginians, including indentured servants of many races, to speak against the Governor. They moved their forces into Jamestown, and the Governor ran. They then set part of Jamestown on fire. The London-based merchant ships, and the British government, sided with Berkeley, and provided him with British soldiers to keep the rebels at bay; the British government took more control from the colonists, suppressing the rebellion.

When the native raiding parties continued to attack, the colonists decided they had had enough. Bacon gathered a large group of men, bringing brandy with him, and after getting them drunk, had them vote him in as the leader. The group rode south into Occaneechi land, convinced them to attack the Susquehannock people, and after they left, murdered those who stayed behind.

The Governor pushed for a new election in the House of Burgess, and Bacon's supporters won, opening their next meeting to pass sweeping rules, called the *Bacon Laws*. He then demanded a militia to defend the frontier and the farmers. The Governor refused his demands and Bacon's 500 men took aim, right for the Governor. Berkeley was unmoved; he simply unbuttoned his shirt, showing his chest, and yelled "shoot." Bacon, in return, told his men to turn their guns on the burgesses and they reluctantly accepted his demands.

Next, in 1676, Bacon wrote the "Declaration of the People," criticizing Berkeley's administration. After nothing came from this Declaration, and the continuous battles, Bacon took his 400-500 men and attacked Jamestown. On September 19, 1676, they captured and burned Jamestown. Before the Royal Navy could arrive to take back Jamestown, Bacon died of dysentery, and though many of his rebels tried to keep it going, it fell apart. Berkeley quickly launched an attack over the river, back into Jamestown, taking the town once again.

In the end, Bacon's estate was forced to side with the British government; many of his supporters were stripped of their property, and Berkeley was forced to resign and sail back to England, where he died shortly after arrival. In an investigation afterwards, it was found that, besides this being the first armed rebellion against the Crown and the government they set up, it was also the first conflict where indentured servants, both black and white, had joined together in open rebellion.

The Jamestown elite knew that a rebellion like this could happen again if they didn't act swiftly. The elite joined together in their efforts, to make white indentured servants less likely to attack in the future, they promised them 50 acres of land when completing their servitude. In an effort to gain favor with the planters, they passed multiple laws allowing them to keep servants longer. They also finally accepted Bacon's plan, and began to push the tribes out of the Virginia colony. As for the black servants that would join a rebellion, the Assembly decided to crush their spirits, by making them lifetime slaves and stripping them of all rights that were previously provided to them by the colonies. The British Parliament agreed with the law and, in 1682, all black servants were turned into slaves-for-life.

Activity: Timeline of Slavery – British laws, having to do with black slaves in North America, were spread out over many years. Here are just some of the dates to consider, among others, just between 1492 and 1700. Your task today is to draw a timeline on a separate sheet of paper, showing when these events took place and their effect. Here are some of the dates to consider:

1492 – Christopher Columbus arrived in Hispaniola;

1500 – Indigenous people were first made slaves;

1542 – Nueva Laws were first signed into law;

1562 – First slave ship departs Africa for South America;

1612 – British begin selling Irish prisoners in America;

1619 – First sale of African servants sold in Virginia;

1655 – John Casor becomes first black lifetime slave without any criminal conviction;

1676 – Virginia black and white indentured servants band together to participate in Bacon's Rebellion;

1680 – Virginia forbids blacks and slaves from bearing arms or congregating, and mandates harsh punishment;

1682 – Virginia and British Parliament declare that all imported black servants are slaves for life;

1684 – New York makes it illegal for slaves to sell goods;

1688 –Pennsylvania Quakers pass the first formal antislavery resolution in the colonies;

1691 – Virginia passes the first law forbidding marriages between whites and blacks, or whites and Natives;

1691 – Virginia prohibits the freeing of slaves within its borders. Free slaves are forced to leave the colony;

1691 – South Carolina passes the first slave codes;

1694 – Rice cultivation is introduced into Carolina. Slave importation increases dramatically;

1696 – Royal African Trade Company loses its monopoly and New England colonists enter the slave trade;

1700 – Pennsylvania legalizes slavery.

Journal Entry: Actual Slavery - We only gave you a small taste of what servitude or slavery would have felt like, without the abuse and harsh conditions you would have had to work in. Now, reflect on what actual slaves, back a few hundred years ago, might have felt, and write it in your journal.

Write your Journal Entry Here:

_____

_____

_____

_____

_____

_____

_____

_____

_____

_____

_____

_____

Conclusion and What You Need to Know (0 – 1700 AD)

There are so many events we may not have spoken of within the first 200 years of the Age of Exploration in the Americas, but these are some of the highlights. Read more on our site, huntthepast.com. These highlights show how important exploration was, and how European exploration especially was crucial to the discovery of the future United States of America. Always take into consideration that most events in history affect other events in history (which affect other events in history…), so learning the context of all events and why they happened is so essential in understanding history.

At this point in American history, you will see that the colonies (those who lived in the Americas) were split, even back to the time of their arrival. Some colonists were loyal to the crowns of the country of their origin, and others wanted to build a society of freedom and equality, separate from their country of origin. Those who came voluntarily were either religious or entrepreneurial, trying to map their own paths. Those who were forcibly shipped to the colonies soon turned to support the colonists who fought against their captors. While there was much disdain for these countries of origin, it is undeniable that they were essential in their role to find and grow these colonies; but, as with all "property," the owners never want to lose their control, and so stepped in to mandate their own laws, even over those set up (and sometimes voted on) by the colonists. When the colonies and the European government's control was threatened, they fought back.

As you will also see, by the turn of the 17th century and the start of the 18th century, the American continent began to change dramatically, and the colonists began fighting to separate themselves from the nations who controlled them. No other area was so adamant for their freedom as the British colonies. The Bacon Rebellion was the first large-scale revolution against the British, but was definitely not the last. North American colonists, as well as those in the Caribbean, the entire Gulf, and most of South America, began to separate themselves from the countries who first claimed them.

This opposition was the start of something much grander in scale, and would start a firestorm around the world. Not one country would be unaffected by what happened next. Be watching for our next book, all about the American Revolution.

Final Journal Entry: Conclusion - This book has also been your journal, throughout this entire 16 week process (or however long you took to work through it). Since we want you to keep this book forever, write your thoughts about what you learned in the next few pages, and then keep this book on your bookshelf to pull out in the future. Don't forget the lessons you learned from this book. Come back to this book often, to remember what you learned and why things happened, especially as you read our follow-up books. After one year, return to this book and spend at least an hour reviewing it; then write your thoughts in the Activity - Part #2 section. There is also additional space to add comments a few years later, as you learn more history and become more knowledgeable of life; so feel free to add additional thoughts and keep this book for the future. Also, I hope you have enjoyed this little adventure through early American History. Stay tuned for more.

Write your Journal Entry (after finishing the book)

_____

_____

_____

_____

_____

_____

_____

_____

_____

_____

_____

_____

_____

_____

_____

Journal Activity – Part #2: (after one year)

_____

_____

_____

_____

_____

_____

_____

_____

_____

_____

_____

_____

_____

_____

_____

Journal Activity – Part #3: (after five years)

_____

_____

_____

_____

_____

_____

_____

_____

_____

_____

_____

_____

_____

Made in the USA
Middletown, DE
24 May 2022

66100919R00156